Business
IN ENGLISH

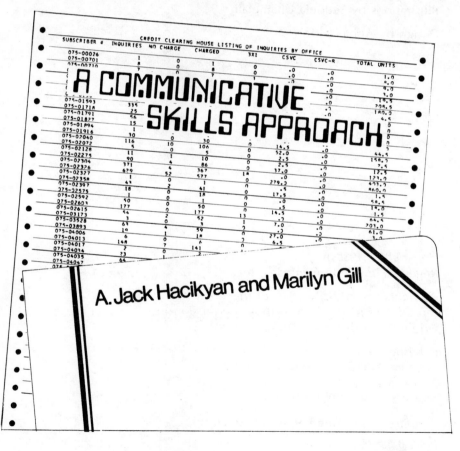

A COMMUNICATIVE SKILLS APPROACH

A. Jack Hacikyan and Marilyn Gill

Regents Publishing Company, Inc.

Illustrations by Sedonia Champlain

Design by Anna Veltfort

Published by
Regents Publishing Company, Inc.
2 Park Avenue
New York, N.Y. 10016

Printed in the United States of America
ISBN 0-88345-369-X

CONTENTS

PREFACE

Since we live in a business civilization, it is no wonder that knowledge of the language of business is vital to many and useful to nearly everyone. With this fact in mind, we address this book to high school, college, and adult students of English at the intermediate or advanced levels. The language of business is something they cannot afford to ignore. At the same time, this book aims at teaching the English spoken in everyday life, avoiding the kind of artificial language so often found in textbooks.

The dialogues of BUSINESS IN ENGLISH were initially prepared at the Center for Applied Linguistics of the University of Franche Comté by M. and W. Alexander. After a long period of testing and consultation, they were completely modified, brought up to date, and rewritten by the present authors. Dialogue summaries were added and exercises were devised to accompany the texts. Throughout the preparation process, particular attention was given to using the language of real-life situations. This explains the emphasis on common idiomatic expressions, prepositional phrases, and phrasal verbs, which are stumbling blocks for every student of English.

It is hoped that this closely integrated and highly practical approach will benefit all students of English.

A. Jack Hacikyan
and
Marilyn Gill

INTRODUCTION

Each of the 25 units in this book contains a dialogue illustrating the use of English in everyday business situations, followed by a series of oral and written exercises. The dialogues tell the story of Mr. Bill Roy, a businessman at Allgood Engineering Company, as he faces a series of situations (some of them surprising, some of them disappointing) while setting up new outlets for his company's products in the United States and abroad. Each dialogue presents a number of commonly used business terms, always in a natural context. When relevant to the dialogue, realia, such as a résumé, a letter of application, or a letter of complaint, is used to enhance the students' knowledge of typical business terminology and procedures.

The business vocabulary and some of the grammar structures used in the dialogues are reviewed in the exercises which follow. These exercises are varied: comprehension questions, vocabulary and grammar reviews, substitution drills, role-playing, and writing activities. The structured exercises help prepare students for the communicative role-playing at the end of each unit.

The glossary and answer key at the back of the book make it possible to use this text for self-instruction. The answer key also provides grammatical explanations for particularly difficult exercises. Students should be encouraged to check their answers with those in the answer key. The authors believe that self-correction helps students develop independence and self-confidence during the learning process.

The text is accompanied by a set of cassette recordings. Each of the 25 dialogues has been recorded. The dialogues are first read in their entirety at normal conversation speed so that students can become accustomed to typical speech. They are then read a second time, but with a pause after each sentence to give students a chance to repeat.

TO THE TEACHER

The following are suggestions for presenting each unit. They are offered bearing in mind that a good teacher will know how to adapt materials to the needs of a particular group of students.

INSTRUCTIONS FOR THE DIALOGUE

1. The short paragraph preceding each dialogue can be used as a listening or reading comprehension activity. Either read it aloud to the students or have them read it silently. Then ask two or three simple questions to make sure that the text has been understood.

2. Play the tape and have students listen to the dialogue with their books open. Then rewind the tape and have students listen to the dialogue a second time with their books closed. (If tapes are not available, read the dialogue to them.) The aim of this is to train students to grasp the content of continuous speech.

3. Have students listen to the second reading of the dialogue, this time with a pause after each sentence for the students to repeat. (If tapes are not available, read the dialogue again and have the students repeat each sentence after you.)

4. Divide the class into pairs. Have each pair read the dialogue and underline the words and phrases they do not understand. The students should try to explain the meanings to each other. This step enables the entire class to participate actively in reading and understanding the passage.

5. Ask the students to point out the words and/or structures they have not understood. Call on other students to help them. If they cannot resolve the problems by themselves, explain the answers to them. Then ask the pairs to act out the dialogue.

6. Have the students read the Dialogue Summary and then ask them to close their books. Have them use the Summary as a departure point to recount the story orally. Either one student can be called on to summarize the entire dialogue or several can contribute to the elaboration of the story.

INSTRUCTIONS FOR THE EXERCISES

Students can work in class, either individually or in pairs, on the exercises which follow each dialogue. The last exercise in each unit is meant to be done outside the classroom, while any of the others may be assigned for homework, if desired.

COMPREHENSION QUESTIONS

Exercise A of each unit consists of several comprehension questions. Its aim is to encourage free oral expression and to insure comprehension. The questions in this section are not exhaustive and others may be added, if desired. Students may also be asked to make up their own questions. An alternative way of using this exercise is as a writing assignment to be done outside the classroom.

If during discussion it becomes clear that some of the business vocabulary in the dialogue has not been fully understood, it should be illustrated by simple examples. Students may be referred to the glossary at the back of the book for definitions of difficult terminology.

Exercise B is a comprehension exercise to enable students to see whether they have understood the details in the dialogue. At the same time it provides a review of the vocabulary within a context.

VOCABULARY REVIEW

Exercise C provides practice in handling new vocabulary, expressions, and prepositions. One of the major reasons why non-English speaking students have difficulty in comprehending spoken English is their lack of mastery of many seemingly unimportant words such as prepositions. These words, which are linguistically situated between items that are purely lexical or purely grammatical, are often not sufficiently reviewed. For this reason emphasis has been given to them in this section.

SUBSTITUTION DRILL

Exercise D is a *cascade* type substitution drill to help students instinctively recognize grammatical categories. It is preferable to have students work in pairs on this exercise so that all of them gain additional practice in oral work. They should take turns making each substitution and should learn to go through this exercise at normal conversation speed. If they experience undue difficulty, the exercise should be repeated until the desired fluency is attained.

GRAMMAR REVIEW

Exercises **E** and **F** (and in some units **exercise G**) are grammar exercises. As mentioned in the preface, this book is for intermediate to advanced level students of English, who have studied English grammar; therefore, instead of giving a systematic review of grammar, these exercises concentrate on specific problem areas. An explanation of the grammatical point being reviewed may be given before having students do the exercise. Each exercise contains an example to be followed. In some cases brief grammatical explanations are given in the answer key.

ROLE-PLAYING

Exercise **G** (in some units **exercise H**) is a role-playing activity. Students choose their own partners and are then given about ten minutes to prepare notes for their presentation. Once they are ready, the class is divided into several groups and each pair of students act out their roles for the others. One or two of the better dialogues should be selected to be performed again, this time in front of the class. This provides a model for the less fluent student and, in general, helps all of them gain more self-confidence when expressing themselves in public.

WRITING

The last exercise in each unit, **exercise H** (in some units **exercise I**), is a writing exercise to be done outside of the classroom. Students should try to use words and expressions contained in the dialogues studied, while developing original ideas. In fact, they should be urged at all times to seek adequate expression for their thoughts, feelings, and experiences. Students must be trained to express themselves in a clear, correct, and concise way. This exercise is a vital part of each unit and is intended to reinforce the initial oral work.

TO THE STUDENT

Business in English has been designed for self-instructional use. The following suggestions will help you use the text for this purpose.

DIALOGUE

Read the short paragraph preceding the dialogue. Then, with your book open, play the tape and listen to the dialogue. Rewind the tape and listen to the dialogue a second time. Let the tape continue. Listen to the dialogue once again, this time repeating each sentence during the pauses. (If tapes are not available, read the dialogue aloud several times.) Refer to the glossary at the back of the book for definitions of any business terms you are unsure of.

Read the Dialogue Summary once or twice. Close your book and try to retell the story orally.

EXERCISES

Answers to all of the exercises, except for the role-playing and writing activities, are given in the answer key at the back of the book. After completing the exercises, be sure to check your answers.

Exercise A Answer the dialogue comprehension questions in complete sentences either orally or in writing.

Exercise B Check your comprehension of the details in the dialogue by choosing the answer which best completes the sentence. Make sure that you have understood all the vocabulary.

Exercise C This exercise provides additional practice in handling the new vocabulary, expressions, and prepositions you have learned.

Exercise D Do this substitution drill orally and as quickly as possible. However, if you experience difficulty, you may wish to write out the answers. This exercise should be repeated several times in order to attain fluency.

Exercises E and **F** (and in some units **exercise G**)   These exercises provide you with a review of specific grammatical problems. Grammar explanations for the more difficult exercises appear in the answer key. If no explanation is given, it means that the grammatical point in guestion is simple enough for you to understand through the examples which are given at the beginning of each exercise.

Exercise G (in some units **exercise H**)   This is a role-playing activity and is intended for the classroom. You may, however, prepare it as if you were to give a classroom presentation.

Exercise H (in some units **exercise I**)   This is a writing exercise. Try to use new vocabulary and expressions in your compositions. Pay special attention to expressing your ideas in clear, correct, and concise sentences.

CAST OF CHARACTERS

In order of appearance

Bill Roy, general manager
Janet Casella, administrative assistant—promoted to assistant marketing
        manager
Jim Jackson, personnel manager
Margaret Smollar, job applicant—hired as administrative assistant
Fred Miller, marketing director
Anna Vilas, comptroller
Rod Milton, advertising manager
Bernie Sutherland, member of the board of directors
Sandra Ravel, plant manager
Ken Ling, shop supervisor
George Tadros, chairman of the board of directors
Elizabeth Kirby, member of the board of directors
Steven Heller, patent attorney for Stopwell Manufacturing, Inc.
Andy Johnson, sales representative
Pat Phillips, assistant comptroller
Judy Lalonde, lawyer representing Allgood
Peter Cook, lawyer—assistant to Judy Lalonde
Doug Oliver, shipping department supervisor
Emil Khan, sales representative
John Williams, sales representative
Claude McAdam, co-owner of McAdam Bros. department store
Peggy Brooks, receptionist

1 | Bill Roy's Working Day

Bill Roy is the general manager of Allgood Engineering, a medium-sized tool manufacturing company based in New York City. He is fifty-seven years old and is a prosperous senior executive. He is also on the board of directors of several other companies. It is nine o'clock in the morning. Bill has just recovered from a cold and is ready to start the day's work.

Characters: Bill Roy, general manager of Allgood
Janet Casella, Bill Roy's administrative assistant

Scene: Bill Roy's office

Bill: Good morning, Ms. Casella.

Janet: Good morning, Mr. Roy. I hope you're feeling better.

Bill: Much better, thank you. What's on the agenda today?

Janet: Mr. Block has an appointment to see you at ten. Then the accountant and, after lunch, your lawyer.

Bill: Which lawyer?

Janet: Mrs. Lalonde.

Bill: Oh—Have the reports come in from the patent bureau?

Janet: Yes. They're on your desk, and I've already sent Mrs. Lalonde her copies.

1

Bill:	Thanks a lot. You're a mind reader. Anything else?
Janet:	Mr. Sutherland has been calling and wants you to return his call.
Bill:	I can't talk to him today. Could you deal with him?
Janet:	Of course. I'll go and get your mail now. *(She exits but then returns and says quietly)* Mr. Ling, the shop supervisor, is here. He says he has to see you immediately.
Bill:	What's the matter now?
Janet:	He says there's trouble in the shop.
Bill:	That does it! I should have stayed in bed. I never have a moment to myself. *(He sighs)* Tell him to come in.

Dialogue Summary

Bill Roy has returned to his office after recovering from a cold. He becomes irritated as his schedule for the day becomes heavier and heavier. A bright spot is Janet Casella's efficient preparation for a meeting with Mrs. Lalonde, one of the lawyers who represents Allgood. But even before Bill has a chance to look at his mail, Mr. Ling, the shop supervisor, arrives unexpectedly to see him.

Exercises

A. Answer these questions about the conversation.

1. Who is Bill Roy?
2. How does he feel about his schedule for the day?
3. How does he deal with Mr. Sutherland?
4. Does Mr. Ling have an appointment to see Bill?
5. Why does he have to see Bill immediately?

B. Select the alternative which best describes what happens in the conversation.

1. Bill Roy is a   a. sales manager.
                    b. shop supervisor.
                    c. general manager.

2. Allgood Engineering is a medium-sized   a. electronics firm.
          b. tool manufacturing company.
          c. advertising agency.

3. Bill Roy is   a. a leading political figure.
              b. a prosperous businessman.
              c. a trade union official.

4. Today Bill is   a. happy to be in the office.
              b. unhappy about his appointments.
              c. indifferent to everything.

5. Janet Casella has sent copies of the report from the patent bureau to   a. the lawyer.
              b. the shop supervisor.
              c. the accountant.

6. a. Janet   is going to deal with Mr. Sutherland.
   b. Mr. Ling
   c. Bill

7. a. A senior executive   arrives without an appointment.
   b. The shop supervisor
   c. The accountant

8. Mr. Ling is having trouble   a. with Bill Roy.
       b. getting an appointment to see
         Bill Roy.
       c. in the shop.

C. Fill in the blanks with the most appropriate word from the right-hand column.

1. I don't have a moment _____ myself.
2. Could you deal _____ Mr. Sutherland?
3. Well, that does _____ !
4. Can I do anything _____ for you?

a. it
b. else
c. with
d. to

5. What's on the _____ today?
6. The shop _____ is waiting.
7. There's a lot of _____ to open.
8. There's trouble in the _____ .

a. supervisor
b. mail
c. shop
d. agenda

9. Bill Roy is a _____ businessman.
10. He's the _____ manager of the company.
11. Bill has become very _____ today.
12. Janet is an _____ assistant.

a. efficient
b. general
c. irritated
d. prosperous

13. Janet is a _____ reader.
14. The _____ of directors meets today.
15. What's the _____ with you?
16. The reports came in from the _____ bureau.

a. patent
b. mind
c. board
d. matter

17. Bill has just _____ from a cold.
18. He hasn't _____ Mr. Sutherland's call.
19. Mrs. Lalonde has _____ the company for two years.
20. Bill should have _____ in bed.

a. returned
b. recovered
c. stayed
d. represented

4

D. Work in pairs. Make new sentences by using the word or phrase from the left column in place of the corresponding part of the preceding sentence. Read the sentences to your partner.

EXAMPLE

	He wants	you	to return	his call.
his pen	He wants	you	to return	his pen.
he would like	He would like	you	to return	his pen.
his money	He would like	you	to return	his money.
to invest	He would like	you	to invest	his money.
us	He would like	us	to invest	his money.

1.

	He says	he has to	see	you	immediately.
tomorrow	He says	he has to	see	you	tomorrow.
he wants to	He says	he wants to	see	you	tomorrow.
discuss it with					
us					
right away					

2.

	Have	the reports	come in from	the patent bureau?
arrived from	Have	the reports	arrived from	the patent bureau?
the main office	Have	the reports	arrived from	the main office?
the statements				
the bank				
haven't				

3.

	The shop	supervisor	is	here.
steward	The shop	steward	is	here.
was	The shop	steward	was	here.
in Detroit				
mechanic				
has been				

4.

	I'll go and	get	your mail	now.
pick up right away send your report find	I'll go and I'll go and	pick up pick up	your mail your mail	now. right away.

E. Ask five questions about the dialogue using the following question words.

EXAMPLE
How is Bill Roy feeling this morning?

1. When _____ ?
2. What _____ ?
3. Which _____ ?
4. Whose _____ ?
5. Why _____ ?

F. Replace the verb *get* **with another verb having the same meaning.**

EXAMPLE
She sent John to *get* the books.
She sent John to pick up the books.

1. Where did you *get* those beautiful stamps?
2. You'll *get* a much better picture with your new television antenna.
3. How much would I *get* if I took the job?
4. I can't *get* clothes that fit me.
5. She *gets* a prize every year for her poems.

G. Act out the following situation with a partner. One partner will take Role 1 and the other will take Role 2. If possible, base your dialogue on an actual work situation.

1. You've just returned from a long business trip. Ask your assistant what happened while you were away. Ask who called, how much work was finished, and what appointments are scheduled for this week.

6

2. Your boss has just returned from a long business trip. Ask about the trip and answer questions about what happened while he or she was away. Try to reassure your boss that everything is all right and that this week's appointment schedule will not be too difficult.

H. Write a short description of yourself similar to the description of Bill Roy on page 1.

Personnel Problems

Bill Roy has gotten through his first day back at work. Now he has to face another disturbing problem, a change in personnel.

Characters: Bill Roy

Jim Jackson, personnel manager

Scene: Bill's office

Bill: Have a seat, Jim. Cigarette?

Jim: No thanks. I don't smoke.

Bill: Of course, I'd forgotten. Well, have you heard the latest?

Jim: You know me, Bill...always too busy to listen to gossip.

Bill: It's not gossip. Mike Edwards has just handed in his resignation. He's leaving us for another company. We can't make him a good enough offer right now.

Jim: That's too bad. He's only been here for a year. I wish he'd been more patient. Oh well, do you have anybody in mind to replace him?

Bill: Well, yes. Janet Casella has always been interested in marketing. She's very sharp and she's in line for a promotion.

8

Jim: Good idea! I think she'd be great in marketing.

Bill: Yes. But it creates another problem. Since Janet started working with me, I've been very spoiled. If she goes, I'll be losing the best administrative assistant I've ever had.

Jim: I understand your problem, Bill. But you'll find another assistant. And look on the bright side: Allgood will be getting a great new assistant marketing manager.

Bill: I suppose you're right. But my vacancy has to be filled immediately. I can't live without an assistant.

Jim: If I place ads in the papers today, we should be able to find a good replacement before the week is out.

Dialogue Summary

Bill Roy tells Jim Jackson about a shift in personnel. He is promoting Janet Casella even though he is concerned about losing her as his assistant. Jim reassures Bill that he'll put ads in the papers immediately, and that they should find a good replacement soon.

Exercises

A. Answer these questions about the conversation.

1. What does Bill Roy mean by "have you heard the latest?"
2. Why has Mike Edwards resigned?
3. Why is Jim Jackson pleased about Janet Casella's promotion?
4. Why is Janet's promotion a problem for Bill?
5. What position are they advertising in the newspapers?

B. Select the alternative which best describes what happens in the conversation.

1. Jim Jackson is employed at Allgood as
   a. the personnel manager.
   b. the marketing manager.
   c. an administrative assistant.

2. Bill Roy and Jim are
   a. acquaintances.
   b. colleagues.
   c. brothers.

3. Jim
   a. smokes a lot.
   b. smokes a pipe.
   c. never smokes.

4. Jim says that he
   a. always
   b. never
   c. sometimes
   listens to gossip.

10

5. Jim is   a. annoyed   that Janet is going to be promoted.
            b. pleased
            c. disturbed

6. Jim thinks that Bill's attitude is   a. unreasonable.
                                    b. annoying.
                                    c. understandable.

7. Mike Edwards is Allgood's   a. chief sales representative.
                            b. assistant marketing manager.
                            c. assistant personnel manager.

8. Bill and Jim decide to   a. look up the ads in the newspapers.
                       b. go and buy some newspapers.
                       c. put ads in the newspapers.

C. Fill in the blanks using the most appropriate word from the right-hand column.

1. He never listens to _____ .   a. line
2. He's handed in his _____ .   b. gossip
3. She's in _____ for a promotion.   c. ad
4. Place an _____ in the papers today.   d. resignation

5. He possesses the necessary _____ .   a. seat
6. The _____ has been filled.   b. offer
7. We can't make him a good enough _____ .   c. vacancy
8. Have a _____ , Jim.   d. skills

9. He's _____ another problem.   a. losing
10. The change in personnel is _____ .   b. working
11. He's been _____ here for a year.   c. facing
12. She's _____ her assistant.   d. disturbing

13. _____ must have experience.   a. personnel
14. Please report to the _____ department.   b. mind
15. I knew about the _____ in personnel.   c. candidates
16. That's just what I had in _____ .   d. shift

17. Look _____ the bright side.   a. for
18. They'll be good _____ marketing.   b. about
19. He's leaving _____ another job.   c. on
20. She's concerned _____ losing her assistant.   d. in

D. Work in pairs. Make new sentences by using the word or phrase from the left column in place of the corresponding part of the preceding sentence. Read the sentences to your partner.

1.

	I'm	always	too	busy	to listen to	gossip.
usually complaints tired he's irritated						

2.

	Do you have	anybody	in mind	to replace	him?
her to train does he have somebody to work with					

3.

	I'll be losing	the best	assistant	I've ever	had.
secretary the most efficient known representative the worst					

4.

	You'll	find	a new	assistant.
marketing manager he'll hire receptionist a good				

5.

	The vacancy	has to	be filled	immediately.
must right away the position should now				

E. Form sentences by putting the verb in parentheses in the present perfect tense and adding the adverb which appears in parentheses after each sentence.

EXAMPLE
Jim (work) with an assistant. (always)
Jim has always worked with an assistant.

1. Bill (avoid) a strike. (just)
2. (hear) you the news? (yet)
3. I (see) that report. (never)
4. She's the best assistant I (have). (ever)
5. Bill (read) the mail. (already)

F. Use *for* or *since* in these sentences. Use *since* to indicate a point in time. Use *for* to indicate a period of time.

EXAMPLE
She's lived here ___*for*___ three years.
She's lived here _*since*_ last May.

1. I've been typing _____ nine o'clock.
2. They've been waiting _____ a long time.
3. He's been working in Chicago _____ five years.
4. They've been in Detroit ever _____ they arrived from Europe.
5. I haven't seen her _____ a few weeks.

13

G. Act out the following situation with a partner. One partner will take Role 1 and the other will take Role 2.

1. You're Mike Edwards, the assistant marketing manager, and you've come to tell Bill Roy that you want to leave Allgood at the end of the month. A large company has offered you the position of marketing manager with a much better salary.

2. You're Bill Roy and are surprised that Mike is resigning. He's only been with the company one year. Tell him that you can offer him a 10% raise in salary and ask him to stay with the company. You believe that you'll be able to promote him in a year or two.

H. Write two advertisements.

1. Advertise an attractive position for a translator from English into your native language.

2. Advertise a part-time position for a sales representative in a large industrial firm.

An Interview

                                    610 Mercer Street, Apt. 5N
                                    Brooklyn, New York 11473

                                    June 3, 1980

Advertiser
Box 4301
New York, N. Y. 10036

Dear Sir or Madam:

I would like to be considered for the position of administrative assistant which you advertised in the _Times_ on
June 2, 1980.

As you can see from the enclosed résumé, I have had three
years experience working as an assistant to a senior
executive. I have supervised and carried out numerous
projects and am confident in my ability to work independently.

I was very interested in your advertisement because I am
seeking a position of greater responsibility, with oppor-
tunity for advancement.

I would appreciate an interview at your convenience. You
may reach me at the number listed on my résumé, or at the
following number during business hours: (212) 333-2299.
As I am currently employed, I would appreciate your
confidence in this matter.

                              Sincerely,

                              Margaret D. Smollar
                              Margaret D. Smollar

Enc.

Margaret D. Smollar
610 Mercer Street, Apt. 5N
Brooklyn, New York 11473
(212) 689-2473

EDUCATION   City College of CUNY
                    B.A. - Political Science - June, 1975

EXPERIENCE

   1977-present   Administrative Assistant and Executive
                    Secretary to Vice President - Vitasine
                    Laboratories, Inc., Brooklyn, New York

                    Developed a series of form letters to
                    respond to customer complaints.
                    Organized a system for recording
                    laboratory data pertinent to sales.
                    Present duties include handling a major
                    part of the customer correspondence, and
                    supervising four persons.

   1976-1977   Secretary and Assistant to Chief
                    Accountant - Vitasine Laboratories, Inc.,
                    Brooklyn, New York

                    Handled telephone and written inquiries.
                    Made out payroll. Typed correspondence.
                    Made major contributions to the
                    reorganization of billing system.

   1975-1976   Receptionist and Gal Friday - Alan Morell
                    Advertising Assoc., New York, New York

                    Was responsible for all general office
                    work, which included filing, typing all
                    correspondence, minor bookkeeping, and
                    screening phone calls.

ADDITIONAL   Traveled in US and Mexico. Fluent in
                    Spanish, with working knowledge of German.
                    Interested in jogging, cross-country
                    bicycling, rebuilding antique cars, and
                    skydiving.

                    References available on request.

Bill Roy is reading the sports section of the *New York Times*. He has forgotten that Margaret Smollar is about to arrive for an interview.

Characters: Bill Roy

Janet Casella

Margaret Smollar, applicant for Janet Casella's position

Scene: Bill's office

Janet: *(The intercom buzzes and Janet speaks from the reception desk.)* Ms. Smollar is here to see you.

Bill: Send her in, please. *(He opens his door and they shake hands.)* How do you do, Ms. Smollar? Please come in and sit down.

Margaret: Thank you, Mr. Roy. I'm pleased to meet you.

Bill: *(He speaks to Janet over the intercom.)* Could you bring in Ms. Smollar's papers, please?

Janet: I believe they're on your desk.

Bill: Oh, here they are. That's the trouble around here. My assistant is always putting things in the most unlikely places, so I never know where they are when I need them.

Margaret: I'm sure you have a great deal to think about.

Bill: *(He glances at the papers.)* Ms. Smollar, I've looked over your résumé. You seem to have just the sort of experience we need.

Margaret: I believe I do. I . . .

Janet: *(The intercom buzzes and Janet speaks again.)* Sorry to disturb you. Mr. Clark is on the line. He says he's about to leave for lunch.

Bill: Dick Clark? Okay, I'll take it. *(To Margaret)* Could you excuse me for a minute? I won't be long. *(To Dick Clark)* Hello, Dick? . . . Much better, thanks—those golf lessons are really topnotch. The pro fixed my swing in no time . . .

17

Dialogue Summary

Bill Roy has forgotten about Margaret Smollar's appointment and is not prepared for the interview. He begins to talk to her but then gets a telephone call. He starts to tell his friend Dick Clark about his golf lesson.

Exercises

A. Answer these questions about the conversation.

1. What is Bill Roy doing when Margaret Smollar arrives for her interview?
2. What does Bill complain about during the interview?
3. Has Margaret had the right experience for the job?
4. What does Bill talk about with his friend Dick Clark?

B. Select the alternative which best describes what happens in the conversation.

1. a. Janet Casella   has just arrived for an interview with Bill Roy.
   b. Margaret Smollar
   c. Ken Ling

2. Bill has been reading   a. a novel.
                            b. the sports section of the *Times*.
                            c. a sales report.

3. Bill   a. hasn't been informed about   the interview.
          b. is well prepared for
          c. has forgotten all about

4. Ms. Smollar   a. seems to have the experience Mr. Roy wants.
                  b. isn't suitable for the job.
                  c. has never been an administrative assistant.

5. The interview is interrupted by   a. the personnel manager.
                                      b. Janet, who knocks at the door.
                                      c. a buzz on the intercom.

6. There is a   a. phone call from Bill's friend.
                 b. phone call from the advertising manager.
                 c. telegram from a representative.

7. Mr. Clark is   a. inviting Bill to   lunch.
                   b. about to leave for
                   c. having hamburgers for

8. Bill tells his friend Dick about   a. the company's financial policy.
                                       b. a professional football player.
                                       c. his golf instructor.

C. Fill in the blanks using the most appropriate word from the right-hand column.

1. I feel much _____ , thanks.
2. She's looking for an _____ assistant.
3. He's forgotten about her _____ .
4. I'm _____ that you can do it.

a. administrative
b. better
c. appointment
d. confident

19

5. You may reach me _____ the office.   a. to
6. He's the assistant _____ the general manager.   b. for
7. I'd like to apply _____ the position.   c. at
8. Please send her _____.   d. in

9. She sent her _____ to the personnel department.   a. convenience
10. She has the right _____ for the job.   b. deal
11. He has a great _____ to do.   c. résumé
12. I'd like an interview at your _____.   d. experience

13. What does he think _____ it?   a. very
14. They're _____ her desk.   b. about
15. We won't be _____ long.   c. over
16. Janet spoke _____ the intercom.   d. on

D. Work in pairs. Make new sentences by using the word or phrase from the left column in place of the corresponding part of the preceding sentence. Read the sentences to your partner.

1.

	Bring in	Ms. Smollar's	papers,	please.
résumé find Mr. Smith's application give me				

2.

	I'm sure	you have	a great deal	to think about.
a lot I realize to worry about too much to do				

20

3.

	I've	looked over	your	résumé.
reports checked they've his statistics				

4.

	You	seem to have	just	the sort of	experience
background appear to have the kind of exactly we want					
	we need.				

5.

	Mr. Clark is	about to	leave for	lunch.
work I'm home go ready to				

E. Complete these sentences with *just* (immediate past) or *about to* (immediate future). Leave the rest of each sentence unchanged.

EXAMPLE
The position has _*just*_ been filled.

1. Margaret is _____ arrive for her interview.
2. Janet has _____ put Margaret's papers on the desk.
3. The interview is _____ end.
4. I've _____ examined your qualifications.
5. Bill is _____ phone the personnel manager.

F. Form sentences by putting the verb in parentheses in the correct tense—the present perfect or simple past tense. For an explanation of the use of these tenses, see the Answer Key.

EXAMPLES
She (interview) five applicants yesterday.
She interviewed five applicants yesterday.
We (be) the leading tool manufacturers since the beginning of the year.
We've been the leading tool manufacturers since the beginning of the year.

1. The last time I (see) him (be) just after Christmas.
2. His father (give) him a tape recorder for his birthday.
3. Do you mean to say you never (be) to Washington?
4. What you (say) to him when he (arrive)?
5. I (be) afraid of her ever since I (hear) her arguing with the accountant.
6. We (sign) the contract last week.
7. Last week we (put) a new door on the office.
8. When he (phone) this morning, he (surprise) his colleagues.
9. She (write) articles for that magazine for the past two years.
10. I never (forgive) him for what he (tell) my competitors.

22

G. Act out the following situation with a partner. One partner will take Role 1 and the other will take Role 2.

1. You're applying for a position in the sales department of a toy manufacturing company, and you're being interviewed. You can speak and write English and have worked for a year in the sales department of a candy company.

2. You're the personnel manager of a toy manufacturing company and are interviewing an applicant for a job in the sales department. The person who gets the job will be in charge of the orders from foreign countries and therefore must be able to speak and write English. He or she must also be systematic and orderly and very diplomatic with customers.

H. Write a letter of application for a position that you would like to have. It can be similar to Margaret's letter on p. 15.

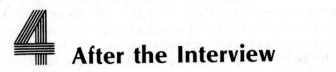

4 After the Interview

Janet Casella and Margaret Smollar are talking outside Bill Roy's office after Margaret's interview.

Characters: Janet Casella
                   Margaret Smollar

Scene: Janet's office

Janet: How did it go?

Margaret: I'm not too sure.

Janet: What makes you say that?

Margaret: Because he didn't really ask me anything. He seemed more interested in his golf than in my interview.

Janet: He's often like that. He seems absent-minded, but don't be fooled. Underneath it all he's quite sharp.

Margaret: Yes, I noticed that. Do you think I have a good chance of getting the job?

Janet: I think so. You sent in an excellent résumé.

Margaret: Thank you. By the way, he had good things to say about your work.

Janet: That was nice of him. Actually he's upset because I'm changing jobs.

Margaret: How long have you been working with him?

Janet: For three years. I might add that it was a very worthwhile experience. Mr. Roy is a good man to work with.

Margaret: I'm sure he is. Well, thank you, Ms. Casella. It was nice meeting you.

Janet: It was nice meeting you, too. And I hope I'll see you here again soon.

Dialogue Summary

Margaret Smollar and Janet Casella are discussing the interview. Margaret thinks that Bill Roy is more interested in golf than in her application, but Janet thinks that Margaret has a good chance of getting the job.

ALLGOOD ENGINEERING COMPANY

875 Greenpoint Avenue   (212) 369-2424
Brooklyn, New York 11219

June 23, 1980

Ms. Margaret D. Smollar
610 Mercer Street Apt. 5N
Brooklyn, N. Y. 11473

Dear Ms. Smollar:

After careful consideration, I am pleased to offer you the position of administrative assistant under the terms we discussed at our meeting.

I would appreciate notification of your decision at your earliest convenience. If you accept, please plan to report to Mr. Jackson, our personnel manager, at 9:00 A.M., on July 7, 1980.

I look forward to working with you and trust our association will be a long and happy one.

Cordially,

William Roy

William Roy
General Manager

WR:kd

Exercises

A. Answer these questions about the conversation.

1. Why isn't Margaret Smollar sure how the interview went?
2. Does Janet Casella think that Bill Roy is absent-minded?
3. Does Janet think that Margaret has a good chance of getting the job?
4. How does Bill feel about Janet's work?
5. How long has Janet been working with him?

B. Select the alternative which best describes what happens in the conversation.

1. Janet is going   a. to travel.
                     b. to be promoted.
                     c. to retire.

2. Margaret and Janet   a. have known each other for a long time.
                            b. have never met.
                            c. have just met.

3. Margaret is   a. convinced   that the interview was a success.
                b. not sure
                c. certain

4. Bill Roy seemed most interested in   a. Margaret's résumé.
                                      b. his golf.
                                      c. Janet's work.

5. Bill is   a. really absent-minded.
            b. easily fooled.
            c. quite sharp.

6. Janet thinks that Margaret   a. will get the job.
                             b. will not get the job.
                             c. will have to apply again.

7. Bill is   a. pleased   about the shift in personnel.
            b. upset
            c. happy

8. Margaret   a. is found unsuitable for the job.
                 b. is told to apply again.
                 c. gets the job.

C. Fill in the blanks using the most appropriate word from the right-hand column.

1. He seemed more _____ in golf.
2. I'm _____ to offer you the position.
3. He's very absent- _____ .
4. Don't be _____ .

    a. minded
    b. interested
    c. fooled
    d. pleased

5. How did _____ go?
6. He's not _____ sure.
7. How long did you work _____ him?
8. That was nice _____ you to say.

    a. of
    b. it
    c. too
    d. with

9. Janet and Margaret are talking _____ Bill's office.
10. I'm looking _____ to hearing from you.
11. He's appreciative _____ your efforts.
12. _____ it all he's a nice man.

    a. of
    b. underneath
    c. forward
    d. outside

13. You _____ very happy today.
14. Margaret wants to _____ jobs.
15. She's got a good _____ of being promoted.
16. You seem quite _____ .

    a. upset
    b. sound
    c. chance
    d. change

D. Work in pairs. Make new sentences by using the word or phrase from the left column in place of the corresponding part of the preceding sentence. Read the sentences to your partner.

1.

	He didn't really	ask	me	anything.
any questions us a single thing tell the truth				

28

2.

	He seemed	more	interested in	his golf.
his problems worried about his board meeting very he was				

3.

	He had	good	things to say about	your work.
wonderful they had your character terrible your friends				

4.

	Do you think	I have	a good chance of
flying to London are you sure he has returning home finding a replacement			
	getting the job?		

5.

	How long	have you been	working	for	him?
has she been her with living since when					

E. Complete the sentences with the appropriate adjective or adverb. Choose from among the following: *long, far, old, big, wide, large, tall, much, many, deep,* **or** *few.*

EXAMPLE
How __*old*__ is the company?

1. How _____ have you been working here?
2. How _____ can you walk in one hour?
3. How _____ are you?
4. How _____ is that river?
5. How _____ is the Empire State Building?
6. How _____ applications were there?
7. How _____ does that car cost?
8. How _____ are your feet?

F. Make sentences by choosing all the possible endings from the right-hand column. There are often several correct combinations. After completing the exercise, study all the possibilities given in the Answer Key.

EXAMPLE

1. *Have you seen them tonight?* (a)
   Have you seen much of her lately? (b)
   Have you seen what he's been doing in the office? (c)

1. Have you seen	a. them tonight?
2. Are you seeing	b. much of her lately?
3. Do you see	c. what he's been doing in the office?
4. Have you been seeing	d. what I mean?
5. They change	a. for dinner right now.
6. They've changed	b. the menu every day.
7. They've been changing	c. a lot recently.
8. They're changing	d. over the past few years.
9. We've got	a. about fifty letters every day.
10. We've been getting	b. information from them for years.
11. We're getting	c. more orders since we started advertising.
12. We get	d. a difficult problem to face.

30

13. They're opening	a. a new store downtown.
14. They've opened	b. too many boxes.
15. They open	c. inquiry letters all morning.
16. They've been opening	d. the store when the tourist bus arrives.

17. I'm going	a. when I can.
18. I've been going	b. home tomorrow.
19. I go	c. there for twenty years now.
20. I've gone	d. for a drive in the country on Sundays.

G. Act out the following situation with a partner. One partner will take Role 1 and the other will take Role 2. If possible, base your dialogue on an actual job that you or your partner has had.

1. You're congratulating a friend on his or her new job. You want to know what kind of job it is, how much your friend earns, what hours he or she works, what his or her boss is like, etc. After you have found out the details, give your friend an opinion about the new job.

2. You're telling a friend about your new job. Tell your friend about your salary, hours, responsibilities, boss, etc.

H. Write a résumé of your background—your education and work experience. Make it similar to Margaret Smollar's résumé on p. 16.

5 Margaret's First Day

Margaret has just arrived for her first day of work at Allgood.

Characters: Jim Jackson, personnel manager
Bill Roy, general manager
Fred Miller, marketing director
Margaret Smollar, Bill's new assistant
Anna Vilas, comptroller
Rod Milton, advertising manager

Scene: Bill's office

Jim: Hello, Bill. I understand you're having a meeting.
May I interrupt it?

Bill: Certainly, Jim. We were just finishing up, anyway.

Jim: I have Ms. Smollar with me. She's ready to start
work.

Bill: Good. You couldn't have come at a better time, Jim.
Show her in. She can meet some of the team.
(Margaret walks in.) I'd like you to meet Margaret
Smollar, my new assistant. Ms. Smollar, this is Fred
Miller, our marketing director.

32

Fred:	Pleased to meet you, Ms. Smollar. *(They shake hands.)* I must say I've heard a lot about you. I hope you'll be happy here.
Margaret:	Thank you, Mr. Miller. That's very kind of you.
Bill:	And this is Anna Vilas, our comptroller.
Anna:	How do you do? *(They shake hands.)*
Margaret:	How do you do?
Bill:	And Rod Milton, our advertising manager.
Rod:	Good morning, Ms. Smollar. Glad to have you with us. *(They shake hands.)*
Margaret:	Thank you. I'm glad to be here.

Dialogue Summary

When Margaret arrives for her first day at work, the personnel manager takes her to Bill's office, where she is immediately introduced to the management team.

Exercises

A. Answer these questions about the conversation.

1. Did Jim know that there was a meeting in Bill's office?
2. Has Jim come at a good time? Why?
3. Who introduces Margaret to the Allgood team?
4. Who is at the meeting, and what position does each have in the company?

B. Select the alternative which best describes what happens in the conversation.

1. Margaret Smollar is   a. shown around the factory.
      b. asked to sit down in the waiting room.
      c. introduced to the management team.

2. The meeting is   a. just starting.
      b. just finishing.
      c. going to continue.

3. Bill thinks that Jim and Margaret have come at   a. the right time.
      b. a bad moment.
      c. the wrong time.

4. Bill is   a. annoyed because Margaret is late.
      b. angry because Margaret has interrupted the meeting.
      c. pleased to introduce his new assistant to his colleagues.

5. Fred has heard   a. a lot about Margaret.
      b. nothing about the shift in personnel.
      c. bad reports about Margaret.

6. Margaret has met   a. all of the management team.
      b. none of the management team.
      c. some of the management team.

7. The   a. marketing director   has heard a lot about Margaret.
      b. advertising manager
      c. comptroller

34

8. Margaret is going to be   a. Fred's   administrative assistant.
                                      b. Bill's
                                      c. Rod's

C. Fill in the blanks using the most appropriate word from the right-hand column.

1. May I _____ you for a minute?   a. meet
2. I'm _____ to meet you.   b. introduce
3. I want to _____ Ms. Smollar to you.   c. pleased
4. I'd like you to _____ my new assistant.   d. interrupt

5. I have Margaret Smollar _____ me.   a. about
6. We've heard a lot _____ you.   b. at
7. I'm glad _____ be here.   c. with
8. This is her first day _____ work.   d. to

9. Margaret met the management _____ .   a. marketing
10. Fred Miller works in _____ .   b. administrative
11. The _____ is in charge of finances.   c. team
12. Margaret is the new _____ assistant.   d. comptroller

13. He took her _____ Bill Roy's office.   a. up
14. They're just finishing _____ the meeting.   b. in
15. You couldn't have come _____ a better time.   c. at
16. Please show Ms. Smollar _____ .   d. to

D. Work in pairs. Make new sentences by using the word or phrase from the left column in place of the corresponding part of the preceding sentence. Read the sentences to your partner.

1.

	May	I	interrupt	your	meeting?
conversation could we speech listen to					

2.

prepared they're they aren't the project to begin	She's	ready	to start	work.

3.

she left moment worse called	You	couldn't have	come	at a	better	time.

4.

nice that was really thoughtful of him	That's	very	kind	of you.

5.

happy in the company delighted I'm them	We're	glad	to have	you	with us.

E. Give synonyms for the following words.

1. to telephone
2. to mail
3. to produce
4. whether
5. top management (positions)

F. Fill in the blanks with the correct form of *say* **or** *tell.*

EXAMPLE
Margaret __told__ Janet what Bill Roy had __said__ to her in the interview.

1. Janet could not _____ Margaret whether she would get the job or not.
2. Fred _____ Margaret that he had heard a lot about her.
3. Rod _____ good morning to Margaret and _____ her that he was glad to have her at Allgood.
4. Margaret _____ that she was glad to be there.
5. Everyone _____ pleasant things to Margaret.

G. Put the verbs in parentheses into the correct tense—the simple past or the past progressive (-ing) tense.

EXAMPLE
The shipment (arrive) while Janet (open) the morning mail.
The shipment arrived while Janet was opening the morning mail.

Bill: I hope that you (have) a chance to talk to Ms. Casella while you (wait) to be introduced to the management team.

Margaret: She (show) me around the office when Mr. Jackson (come) to introduce me to everyone.

Bill: Good. I (ask) her to do that yesterday while we (make) a list of unfinished projects. So now you know something about our office procedures.

Margaret: Actually, not much. While she (explain) things to me, the phone (ring), and she (have) a long conversation with someone. Then, when she (begin) to tell me a few more things, the door (open) and Mr. Jackson (come) out to get me.

H. Act out the following situation with three other people.

1. You're George Mullen, the president of Reelbad Manufacturers. Mike Edwards, the new marketing manager of your company, has just been shown into your office. You're meeting with Barbara Howard, the advertising manager, and David Valente, a lawyer. This is a good time for him to meet them. You make the proper introductions.

2. You're Barbara Howard, the advertising manager. George Mullen has told you a lot about Mike Edwards. You'll be working closely with him. Tell him you're happy to welcome him to Reelbad.

3. You're David Valente, a lawyer. Your firm has represented Reelbad for many years. Tell Mike Edwards you're pleased to meet him.

4. You're Mike Edwards, the new marketing manager of Reelbad. You've just been shown into George Mullen's office. You're being introduced to two people that you'll be working with. You want to make a good first impression.

I. Pretend that you are Margaret Smollar. Write a letter to a friend telling him or her about your first day of work at Allgood.

Work Efficiency at Allgood

Bill Roy senses a possible conflict between the senior and junior executives of the company. It would be a serious problem if the managers formed two separate camps. He needs more information in order to deal with the situation effectively.

Characters: Bill Roy

Jim Jackson

Scene: Bill's office

Bill: Jim, I suspect something's going on that I don't know about.

Jim: What do you mean?

Bill: Well, it seems to me that our junior people have had something on their minds lately.

Jim: I've heard a couple of things here and there . . . but we're probably talking about different things.

Bill: Come off it, Jim. Tell me what's going on.

Jim: Okay. Just the other day I was having lunch with some of the staff. They were all saying what a nice boss you were to work for.

39

Bill: That's a nice little story. But I want to know what's going to happen at the policy meeting.

Jim: What about putting *your* cards on the table?

Bill: I will, if it means you'll tell me what you know.

Jim: It's a deal. *(He pauses)* Our eager-beaver junior executives seem to have been bitten by an "efficiency bug."

Bill: So, I was right.

Jim: But I don't see anything wrong with that.

Bill: I'm not too sure, Jim. Right now, I think there's room for improvement. But I think it's the wrong time to make any significant changes.

Dialogue Summary

Bill Roy calls Jim Jackson into his office to ask him about the upcoming policy meeting. Although Jim treats it lightly, Bill is still worried about the conflict between his senior and junior managers.

Exercises

A. Answer these questions about the conversation.

1. Why does Bill Roy suspect that something is going on?
2. What does Bill want to know?
3. What does Jim Jackson mean by "putting your cards on the table?"
4. Do you think that Jim is on the side of the junior or the senior executives?
5. How does Bill feel about this "efficiency bug"?

B. Select the alternative which best describes what happens in the conversation.

1. Bill Roy   a. doesn't have any   problems at the office.
              b. has never had any
              c. has

2. Bill is concerned about   a. a card game.
                       b. being bitten by a dangerous bug.
                       c. a possible conflict in the team.

3. Bill called   a. Fred Miller   in to talk things over.
            b. Jim Jackson
            c. Rod Milton

4. Jim has heard   a. many things.
               b. nothing.
               c. a couple of things.

5. Bill wants Jim to   a. tell him a story.
                  b. tell him what's going on.
                  c. invite him to lunch.

6. Bill decides to   a. put his cards on the table.
               b. play cards.
               c. deal cards.

7. Bill doesn't think   a. there's room for improvement.
                  b. it's the right time to make changes.
                  c. he'll put his cards on the table.

8. Jim appears to be
   a. very worried about the policy meeting.
   b. in agreement with the junior executives.
   c. very anxious to play cards.

C. Fill in the blanks using the most appropriate word from the right-hand column.

1. They have something _____ their minds.
2. There's room _____ improvement.
3. He couldn't deal _____ the situation.
4. I don't know _____ that.

a. with
b. about
c. for
d. on

5. I suspect _____'s going on.
6. Tell me exactly _____ happened.
7. I don't see _____ wrong.
8. I've heard a _____ of things.

a. couple
b. anything
c. something
d. what

9. She's not _____ sure.
10. He _____ his cards on the table.
11. I saw him _____ the other day.
12. Bill _____ there was a problem.

a. put
b. just
c. too
d. sensed

13. We had lunch with some of the _____ .
14. The managers formed separate _____ .
15. She's a nice _____ to work for.
16. It's a _____ !

a. boss
b. deal
c. staff
d. camps

17. He's worried about the _____ meeting.
18. It's not possible to make _____ changes.
19. The _____ executives are efficient.
20. The junior executives formed a _____ camp.

a. policy
b. separate
c. junior
d. significant

42

D. Work in pairs. Make new sentences by using the word or phrase from the left column in place of the corresponding part of the preceding sentence. Read the sentences to your partner.

1.

	I suspect	something	's going on.
's happening I think he thinks could happen anything			

2.

	They've had	something	on their minds
a lot too much recently to think about for some time now			
	lately.		

3.

	I've	heard	a couple of	things.
rumors a number of they've started projects				

4.

	I think	there	's	room for	improvement.
I feel she feels a chance for advancement could be					

5.

	It's	the wrong time	to make	any	changes.
improvements to authorize those the right time it was					

E. Fill in the blanks with the infinitive or the -ing form of the verb.

EXAMPLE
The board considered _changing_ the location of the company. (change)

1. She finished _____ for Allgood in February. (work)
2. Until now, they avoided _____ shipments by air. (send)
3. We hope _____ to the meeting this afternoon. (go)
4. She enjoys _____ the market reports. (read)
5. He planned _____ the order. (cancel)
6. Did you expect _____ a license? (get)
7. We've decided _____ this very carefully. (discuss)

F. Fill in the blanks using to put **or** to take **in the correct tense.**

EXAMPLE
The company really __put__ on a show at the Trade Fair last year.

1. Since it's late, I'll _____ off answering the letters until tomorrow.

2. Look, the Concorde has just _____ off!
3. _____ the week off and have a good rest.
4. It rained so much that the match had to be _____ off.
5. As there's nothing else to do, I'll _____ off.
6. They _____ the lights back on last night.
7. They always _____ off their coats when they enter the building.

G. Act out the following situation with a partner. One partner will take Role 1 and the other will take Role 2.

1. You are a good friend of a famous person. You know a secret about the person: he or she is getting fired/getting married/getting divorced/has been arrested/is going to climb Mt. Everest. You don't want anyone to know the secret, or even to know that there is a secret, at least for a while.

2. You are a gossip columnist. You know something is going on with a certain famous person. You suspect that the good friend of this person knows what is happening. Try to find out what's going on. Make a deal if you have to.

H. Write a paragraph about a conflict that you have experienced at work or at school.

7 The Efficiency Study

It is now a few days later, and Bill Roy is about to adjourn the policy meeting.

Characters:	Bill Roy, general manager
	Anna Vilas, comptroller
	Bernie Sutherland, member of the board of directors
	Sandra Ravel, plant manager
	Jim Jackson, personnel manager
	Rod Milton, advertising manager
	Fred Miller, marketing director

Scene: The board room

Bill: Now, that takes care of all matters on the agenda. Does anyone want to raise anything else before I adjourn the meeting?

Anna: Yes. I've been looking at some of the figures from last quarter and I have some questions regarding the company's efficiency.

Mr. Sutherland: This is definitely a matter for serious discussion.

Anna: I think we need more than just a discussion,

	Mr. Sutherland. I'm suggesting that the company would benefit from an efficiency study done by an outside team of consultants.
Sandra:	Efficiency study! There isn't any need for that. Look, if we'd all get back to work instead of sitting here talking, it would increase everyone's productivity.
Jim:	I agree with you, Sandra; but it may not be a bad idea to have some outside opinions.
Sandra:	And what about the rest of the staff? I'm sure none of our workers will like the idea. *And* I remember ICA Engineering had a serious strike on its hands as a result of an efficiency study.
Rod:	That was because of poor labor relations.
Anna:	The survey only sparked off the trouble, Sandra.
Mr. Sutherland:	Before we waste any more time talking about the proposal, I suggest we put it to a vote.
Fred:	Not yet, Mr. Sutherland. I think some more discussion is in order.
Bill:	I agree. But it's getting late, and I don't think we can resolve this issue to our satisfaction today. I therefore will call a special meeting on this matter for Thursday at 3:00 P.M.

Dialogue Summary

The policy meeting is just ending when Anna Vilas suggests bringing in a team of consultants to conduct an efficiency study. However, Sandra Ravel is worried about the workers, who may react negatively to such outside intrusion. There is some discussion among the members. Then Bill decides to call a special meeting.

Exercises

A. Answer these questions about the conversation.

1. Was the question concerning the company's efficiency on the agenda?
2. Who is in favor of the study? Why?
3. Who is not in favor of the study? Why?

B. Select the alternative which best describes what happens in the conversation.

1. The idea of an efficiency study is brought up at a
   a. private meeting.
   b. policy meeting.
   c. union meeting.

2. The management team   a. always does what Bill wants.
   b. always votes unanimously.
   c. has different opinions.

3. Anna Vilas doesn't think the problem of efficiency will be solved by
   a. a survey.
   b. a meeting.
   c. a discussion.

4. a. All of   the members are in favor of Anna's proposal.
   b. Not all of
   c. None of

5. Sandra Ravel thinks efficiency will be improved by
   a. efficient plant management.
   b. talking.
   c. returning to work.

6. Jim Jackson is   a. for   the survey.
                    b. against
                    c. undecided about

7. The ICA survey resulted in   a. better efficiency.
                          b. a strike.
                          c. improved engineering.

8. The management team, as a whole, thought that Anna's proposal   a. was an excellent idea.
                                          b. was not good.
                                          c. needed to be discussed.

C. Fill in the blanks using the most appropriate word from the right-hand column.

1. What _____ the rest of the staff?   a. for
2. What's _____ the agenda today?   b. with
3. There isn't any need _____ that.   c. on
4. I agree _____ you.   d. about

5. That takes _____ of the matter.   a. some
6. The survey _____ sparked off the trouble.   b. else
7. _____ more discussion is in order.   c. care
8. Is there anything _____ we must discuss?   d. only

9. We must bring _____ an outside expert.   a. on
10. ICA had a strike _____ its hands.   b. off
11. That was because _____ poor management.   c. in
12. The survey only sparked _____ the trouble.   d. of

13. It's on the _____ .   a. quarter
14. We'll hire a team of _____ .   b. efficiency
15. These are the figures from last _____ .   c. agenda
16. It's a question of the company's _____ .   d. consultants

17. Don't _____ any more time.   a. get
18. Shall we _____ the meeting?   b. waste
19. It will _____ productivity.   c. adjourn
20. Let's _____ back to work.   d. increase

49

D. Work in pairs. Make new sentences by using the word or phrase from the left column in place of the corresponding part of the preceding sentence. Read the sentences to your partner.

1.

	That takes care of	all	the items
most of the topics a few of Let's discuss in the report			
	on the agenda.		

2.

	I have	some	questions	regarding
about a few I want to ask the company's policy they posed				
	the company's efficiency.			

50

3.

	This is	definitely	a matter	for	serious
a topic certainly thoughtful obviously debate					
	discussion.				

4.

	That was	because of	poor	labor	relations.
the result of staff due to cooperation excellent					

5.

	The survey	only	sparked off	the trouble.
the battle merely the report added to the problem				

E. Fill in the blanks with *some or any.*

EXAMPLE
There isn't __any__ carbon paper in the drawer.

1. _____ telephones are black and _____ are white.
2. Call the repair shop—hardly _____ of the machines are working.
3. You'll be expected to answer at least _____ of the questions.
4. There aren't _____ envelopes in the supply room.
5. When _____ of the representatives arrived, we realized it was Wednesday.
6. _____ of the executives have already left.
7. There are never _____ interesting magazines in the waiting room.
8. Luckily I was asked _____ of the questions I had prepared.
9. There is hardly _____ coffee left.
10. I don't think I'll ever get _____ better at typing.

F. Fill in the blanks with one of the following:

somebody	somewhere	something
anybody	anywhere	anything
nobody	nowhere	nothing

EXAMPLE
Sorry, but there's __nothing__ more that we can do; it's completely broken.

1. He told me _____ about the job—not even how much it pays.
2. Unless we tell them _____ about the new procedures, they won't know how to begin the project.
3. He always stays at home; he never goes _____ .
4. Barbara is working _____ in Canada—Quebec, I think.
5. He didn't say _____ after the interview—not a word.
6. _____ delivered this package. Who was it?
7. She's new here and hasn't met _____ yet—not even the receptionist.

G. Act out the following situation with a partner. One partner will take Role 1 and the other will take Role 2.

1. You're the general manager of a toy factory. You want to improve the efficiency of your operation. You know the workers waste a lot of time because of the old-fashioned machinery and because they do a lot of

the work by hand. You want to replace the old-fashioned machinery with new equipment. But the only way for you to buy new equipment is to lay off some workers. You call in the production manager, explain the situation, and tell him or her to prepare to lay off about half of the workers. You want this done in one month.

2. You're the production manager. You're very upset when the general manager tells you about the upcoming layoff. You know that you can't maintain the same level of quality using new machinery and fewer workers. Try to explain to him or her that the new machines don't do as good a job as the skilled craftsmen you now employ. Also, part of the work can only be done by hand. Try to change his or her mind, or if not, then reach a compromise if you can.

H. Write a summary of the speech you are going to give at the next board meeting asking for one of the following:

1. New equipment and permission to lay off some workers.

2. That none of the workers be replaced by machinery. Mass production will ruin the quality of your product.

The Study Creates a Problem

The board approved the efficiency study at the special meeting. Although all the employees at Allgood have been told about the study, this doesn't mean that it will proceed without trouble.

Characters: Margaret Smollar
Bill Roy
Ken Ling, shop supervisor

Scene: Bill's office

Margaret: Excuse me, Mr. Roy. The shop supervisor says he's got to see you immediately.

Bill: That means trouble. Send him in. *(Ken Ling enters.)* Please sit down, Mr. Ling. What do you want to see me about?

Ken: It's about a guy with a stopwatch and calculator who showed up at the plant this morning.

Bill: That must be Art Shafer, the head of the team of consultants.

Ken: I don't care who he is, but he's been breathing down my neck for two hours, and I don't like it.

Bill: I'm sorry about that, but you were told all about the study.

Ken: Yes, but I didn't expect *this*.

Bill: What does Ms. Ravel say about it?

Ken: Nothing. I haven't talked to her.

Bill: You haven't talked to the plant manager? Why not? Don't you know the proper procedures?

Ken: Okay. I made a mistake. But you can tell me off later, Mr. Roy. The point is that the workers don't like the study any more than I do. And they're ready to walk off the job.

Bill: And *you* waited until the last minute to do something! *(He speaks to Margaret over the intercom.)* Ms. Smollar, please tell Ms. Ravel to come here immediately. We've got a mess on our hands. Look, Mr. Ling. Do you know what plant managers are for? They help keep little problems from turning into big ones.

Dialogue Summary

Ken Ling, the shop supervisor, has come to Bill Roy with a problem: the workers don't like the way the efficiency study is being conducted and are threatening to walk off the job. Bill is angry because Ken hasn't talked to the plant manager. He tells Ken that he should have called her immediately, and arranges for her to come to his office.

Conclusion

With the help of Sandra Ravel, the plant manager, Bill Roy calms his workers down, and production returns to normal. The study is finished with no further problems. The team of experts' final report includes valuable suggestions for improving production. Bill can put some of them into effect immediately.

Exercises

A. Answer these questions about the conversation.

1. Why has Ken Ling come to see Bill Roy?
2. Who is the man with the stopwatch and calculator?
3. Was Ken told about the efficiency study?
4. Has Ken talked to Sandra Ravel about his problem?
5. What are the workers ready to do?
6. What is the final result of the efficiency study?

B. Select the alternative which best describes what happens in the conversation.

1. Bill Roy is told that the   a. survey expert   wants to see him.
                                     b. secretary
                                     c. shop supervisor

2. Ken Ling's visits usually mean   a. an excuse for a conversation.
                                       b. trouble.
                                       c. good news.

3. Ken   a. is bored.
          b. wants to tell Bill a new joke.
          c. is angry.

4. a. The personnel manager   showed up at the plant that morning.
   b. The plant manager
   c. The head of the team
      of consultants

5. Bill   a. knows Ken hasn't   been informed about the study.
         b. doesn't think Ken has
         c. knows Ken has

6. Ken   a. hasn't consulted the plant manager.
         b. expected Art Shafer to breathe down his neck.
         c. hoped Sandra would talk to him.

7. The workers don't like   a. to study efficiently.
                      b. Sandra Ravel.
                      c. the efficiency study.

C. Fill in the blanks using the most appropriate word from the right-hand column.

1. What did she _____ to you?   a. breathe
2. What do you _____ to see me about?   b. say
3. I don't _____ who he is.   c. want
4. I don't like people to _____ down my neck.   d. care

5. What are the proper _____ ?   a. calculator
6. He's a member of the team of _____ .   b. point
7. Who is that man with a _____ ?   c. procedures
8. The _____ is that the workers are upset.   d. consultants

9. You can tell me _____ later.   a. for
10. They don't like it any _____ than I do.   b. about
11. Do you know what they're used _____ ?   c. off
12. You were told all _____ it.   d. more

13. Don't wait _____ the last minute.   a. on
14. The workers want to walk _____ the job.   b. up
15. He showed _____ this morning.   c. off
16. We've got a mess _____ our hands.   d. until

D. Work in pairs. Make new sentences by using the word or phrase from the left column in place of the corresponding part of the preceding sentence. Read the sentences to your partner.

1.

	He says	he's got to	see you	immediately.
right now speak to you he has to he claims as soon as possible				

2.

	It's about	a guy	who showed up	at the plant
a woman last year who worked a doctor in the hospital				

this morning.

3.

	That	must be	the head of
the company may be the director of he the project			

the team of consultants.

4.

	He's been	breathing down my neck
bothering me all day long they've been since this morning annoying us		
	for two hours.	

5.

	Don't you	know	the proper	procedures?
the correct doesn't he method didn't she learn				

E. Complete the sentences with the present tense of either *do* or *make*.

EXAMPLE
My boss *does* my worrying for me.

1. My secretary _____ my decisions for me.
2. My sales manager _____ my thinking for me.
3. My children _____ life difficult for me.
4. My husband _____ the shopping for me.
5. My chauffeur _____ my driving for me.
6. My rival _____ trouble for me.
7. My representative _____ the same mistakes I do.
8. My children _____ a lot of noise and disturb me.

F. Fill in the blanks with an appropriate preposition.

EXAMPLE
Is that the package it came _in_ ?

1. Who will I give this book _____ ?
2. What's it used _____ ?
3. Who are they laughing _____ ?
4. What was he referring _____ ?
5. What are these coins made _____ ?
6. Is that salary enough to live _____ ?
7. Is he the friend you went to Paris _____ ?
8. Is it worth worrying _____ ?

G. Act out the following situation with a partner. One partner will take Role 1 and the other will take Role 2.

1. You're an administrative assistant. Your boss has asked you to stay at work late to finish up a very urgent job. You can't stay because you've promised to go to your mother's birthday party. You feel you could have finished the job earlier, but your boss never told you what the deadline was.

2. You're the boss. This job must be finished because you're leaving first thing in the morning on a business trip and you have to take the job with you. You forgot to tell your assistant about the deadline, but you feel that he or she should have asked about it.

H. Describe in 100 words what Ken Ling saw in the plant this morning. Make definite references to Art Shafer and his efficiency study.

An Advertising Campaign

Allgood is preparing to manufacture a brand new line of screwdrivers and wrenches. Rod Milton and his team have been working on an advertising campaign to introduce the new line. Bill Roy wants to know the details before the campaign is presented to the board of directors, and has called Rod in for a meeting.

Characters: Bill Roy

Rod Milton

Scene: Bill's office

Bill: Good afternoon, Rod. You've got the new advertising campaign all worked out now, haven't you?

Rod: Yes, I have. It's going to revolutionize the company's image.

Bill: Wonderful! Tell me about it.

Rod: This is the strategy. We'll have a saturation campaign through the media: radio and TV spots, display ads in newspapers and trade journals . . . the works! And the initial exposure will be an exhibit at the trade fair in Chicago next month.

Bill: The trade fair . . . Yes, I like that idea. But as for the rest, I don't know. Don't forget there's a limit on how much we can spend.

Rod: Of course. But wait till you hear the details. I know you'll like the radio spot. We've got a jingle that will make Allgood a household word.

Bill: Rod, I'm afraid we're not seeing eye to eye on this. I don't think Allgood needs to become a household word. We don't even sell directly to the public.

Rod: *(With disappointment in his voice)* Are you sure you want me to go on, Bill? It seems that you've already decided what to do.

Bill: Don't get excited, Rod. Just remember we have budget restrictions, that's all.

Dialogue Summary

Rod Milton is explaining his advertising campaign to Bill Roy. Bill is concerned with both the quality of the campaign and the limits on the company's budget. Unfortunately, Rod does not understand this, and feels that Bill is overlooking the value of his ideas.

Exercises

A. Answer these questions about the conversation.

1. What is Rod's advertising strategy?
2. Why isn't Bill in favor of the general strategy?
3. Why is Bill against jingles (singing commercials)?
4. Why is Rod disappointed by Bill's reaction?

B. Select the alternative which best describes what happens in the conversation.

1. Rod Milton and his team have been asked to
    a. design a new product.
    b. create a new brand image.
    c. prepare an advertising campaign.

2. The campaign is to
    a. promote the new line.
    b. sell more washing detergent.
    c. beat the competition.

3. Bill Roy
    a. dislikes
    b. is uncertain about
    c. likes
    the idea of the trade fair.

4. Bill is
    a. in favor of
    b. indifferent to
    c. against
    the idea of radio advertising.

5. Rod
    a. would like
    b. didn't want
    c. hadn't expected
    Allgood to become a household word.

6. Allgood doesn't sell their products
    a. at trade fairs.
    b. by advertising.
    c. directly to the public.

7. Rod is upset because Bill
    a. can't make up his mind.
    b. has already decided what to do.
    c. sees eye to eye with him.

8. Rod's campaign is   a. within the budget.
                           b. too expensive for the budget.
                           c. in harmony with the budget.

C. Fill in the blanks using the most appropriate word from the right-hand column.

1. It's a saturation campaign through the _____ .   a. strategy
2. It'll change the company's public _____ .   b. exposure
3. This is the _____ for the advertising campaign.   c. image
4. The initial _____ will be at the fair.   d. media

5. Allgood's not a _____ word.   a. display
6. We need a _____ campaign.   b. exhibit
7. We'll have an _____ at the trade fair.   c. saturation
8. Don't you want _____ ads?   d. household

9. We have budget _____ .   a. jingle
10. This _____ will make us a household word.   b. details
11. There's a _____ to what we can spend.   c. restrictions
12. Have you heard all the _____ ?   d. limit

13. We don't sell _____ to the public.   a. out
14. Have you _____ decided what to do?   b. just
15. _____ remember we have a budget.   c. directly
16. You've got it worked _____ now.   d. already

D. Work in pairs. Make new sentences by using the word or phrase from the left column in place of the corresponding part of the preceding sentence. Read the sentences to your partner.

1.

	You've got	the new	advertising campaign	all
figured out next year's she's got budget completely				
	worked out.			

2.

	It's going to	revolutionize	the company's
ruin it will hurt the manager's plan			
	image.		

3.

	There's	a limit on	how much	we can spend.
we can pay how many people we can hire they've put a ceiling on				

4.

	We've got	a jingle	that will make	Allgood
we've thought of famous an idea a fortune that could cost us				
	a household word.			

5.

	Are you	sure	you want	me	to go on?
you'd like to continue positive him to finish					

E. In a sentence or two, explain the function of the following people.

1. advertising manager
2. general manager
3. personnel manager
4. comptroller

F. Fill in the blanks with the appropriate preposition. Choose from among the following: *by, to, at, of, on, in, for, about, until.*

EXAMPLE
Notice _to_ all employees: the office will close _at_ 3:00 pm _on_ Friday, and will remain closed _until_ Tuesday morning.

1. I wrote ____ him ____ his account and he replied ____ return mail.
2. It was sold ____ Wilson and Sons, Inc. ____ $400.00 ____ our top representative.
3. Look ____ the TV section and tell me what's ____ TV ____ 8:00 pm ____ Monday evening.
4. The four ____ them left ____ the exhibition ____ high spirits.

G. Make sentences by combining phrases from the right-hand column with the left-hand column. There may be more than one correct combination. After completing the exercise, study all the possibilities given in the Answer Key.

EXAMPLE
He had on _____ .
He had on his best suit for the interview. (h)

1. He put on   _____ .
2. He was on   _____ .
3. He got on _____ .
4. He came on _____ .
5. He went on _____ .
6. He kept on   _____ .

a. at Grand Central Station.
b. talking and we couldn't stop him.
c. the Titanic.
d. the early train from Washington.
e. a play.
f. calling him after he changed jobs.
g. a lot of weight over Christmas.
h. his best suit for the interview.
i. a film about Asia.

H. Act out the following situation with a partner. One partner will take Role 1 and the other will take Role 2.

1. You believe that advertising, whether on TV and radio, or in the newspapers, is really a form of brainwashing. You feel that advertisers make false claims about most products, and that advertising makes the innocent public buy things they do not want or need.

2. You believe that advertising is necessary. You think that most advertisers do their best to tell the truth about their products. It's obvious to you that advertising helps consumers to learn about many different products and to make intelligent choices when they buy.

I. Imagine you are a newspaper reporter who has just interviewed the advertising manager of Allgood. Write a short article of 100-150 words for the business page of the newspaper entitled: "Allgood Markets Brand New Screwdriver."

10 A Board Meeting

Bill Roy and Rod Milton have discussed the advertising campaign and have reached a compromise. Now they are going to present it to the board of directors for approval.

Characters: George Tadros, chairman of the board of directors
Fred Miller, marketing director
Bernie Sutherland, member of the board of directors
Elizabeth Kirby, another member of the board
Bill Roy, general manager
Rod Milton, advertising manager

Scene: The board room

Mr. Tadros: Shall we begin, ladies and gentlemen? I believe you've all had a chance to read the minutes of our last meeting. Shall we accept them as written?

Mr. Sutherland: I make a motion to accept them.

Mrs. Kirby: I second the motion.

Mr. Tadros: All in favor? (*A chorus of "ayes."*) Accepted unanimously. Now, to the business of the day: our new line of screwdrivers and wrenches. It seems that we're about to take the market by storm. Mr. Miller, why don't you take it from here?

Fred:	Thank you, Mr. Tadros. Our research shows there's a great potential market for our new products. As a matter of fact, all we need now is a good promotional push, and we'll expand our marketing horizons way beyond what was expected for this year. And I understand that Mr. Milton has worked out an impressive advertising campaign for us.
Mr. Sutherland:	*(He interrupts.)* I'd like to make a suggestion. Since we're introducing something completely new, I think we need completely new names. We have to show that we're modern, up-to-date, progressive.
Mrs. Kirby:	*(Obviously irritated)* I think we should emphasize the quality and craftsmanship of our products.
Mr. Sutherland:	But we still need new names, and I've come up with some really great ones. How about "Boltwranglers" for the bluejean generation? Or "Startwisters"? —That has a space age sound.
Mrs. Kirby:	May I suggest that we proceed in order and take a look at the proposed campaign first?
Mr. Tadros:	Certainly. If there are no objections, Mr. Milton will proceed to outline the campaign.
Mr. Sutherland:	Couldn't we have some coffee first?
Mr. Tadros:	I believe it'll be here in a minute. Mr. Milton, the floor is yours.
Rod:	Thank you. First, we've developed a few ideas for TV and radio spots, including—
Mr. Sutherland:	*(He interrupts.)* TV and radio spots! Now that's progressive! Incidentally, I've got some really great ideas for commercials.
Bill:	I hate to interrupt you, Mr. Sutherland, but the discussion is going off on a tangent. First, let's get the overall picture. We have to make decisions on the campaign itself. Then we can talk about incidentals.

Dialogue Summary

Mr. Tadros calls the board meeting to order and introduces the subject of the new line of wrenches and screwdrivers. Rod Milton is about to present the new advertising campaign when Mr. Sutherland, a member of the board, interrupts with some of his "great" ideas. Elizabeth Kirby, another member of the board, doesn't like Mr. Sutherland's suggestions at all. The discussion is not making any progress, so Bill Roy finally tries to bring the meeting back to order and convince the board to deal with the topic step by step.

Exercises

A. Answer these questions about the conversation.

1. What is the business of the day?
2. What does the company need to do in order to expand their market?
3. What does Mr. Sutherland think they should do to sell the new line?
4. How does Mrs. Kirby feel about Mr. Sutherland's suggestions?
5. How is the meeting finally brought back to order?

B. Select the alternative which best describes what happens in the conversation.

1. The meeting takes place in   a. the factory.
                                      b. the board room.
                                      c. Bill Roy's office.

2. The minutes are   a. accepted by everyone.
                      b. accepted by only a few board members.
                      c. the most important business of the day.

3. The purpose of the meeting is to present to the shareholders
   a. the new ad campaign.
   b. new brand names.
   c. TV commercials.

4. Fred Miller thinks that Allgood should   a. change their image.
                                      b. expand their markets.
                                      c. emphasize craftsmanship.

5. During the meeting, Mr. Sutherland   a. makes important suggestions.
                                        b. gets the overall picture.
                                      c. goes off on tangents.

6. The board has to make decisions on   a. the campaign itself.
                                      b. which jingles to use.
                                    c. names for screwdrivers.

7. The meeting proceeds   a. in an orderly fashion.
                           b. without interruptions.
                           c. after many interruptions.

8. a. Mr. Tadros   finally brings the meeting back to order.
   b. Bill Roy
   c. Rod Milton

C. Fill in the blanks using the most appropriate word from the right-hand column.

1. Mrs. Kirby _____ the motion.   a. reached
2. Shall we accept the minutes as _____ ?   b. seconded

3. Rod _____ to outline the campaign.   c. written
4. Rod and Bill had _____ a compromise.   d. proceeded

5. Our products are modern in _____ .   a. line
6. Don't go off on a _____ .   b. day
7. Now to the business of the _____ .   c. tangent
8. It's our new _____ of screwdrivers.   d. design

9. She's worked _____ a campaign for us.   a. with
10. We're _____ to date.   b. out
11. They've come up _____ a good name.   c. for
12. What are your ideas _____ TV spots?   d. up

13. There's a great _____ market for our products.   a. push
14. The company needs a good promotional _____ .   b. horizons
15. Let's emphasize the _____ of our products.   c. potential
16. Our marketing _____ are greater than we   d. craftsmanship
    expected.

17. I've _____ some really great ideas.   a. taken
18. We haven't _____ any coffee yet.   b. got
19. The board hasn't _____ any decisions.   c. made
20. They haven't _____ a look at the campaign.   d. had

D. **Work in pairs. Make new sentences by using the word or phrase from the left column in place of the corresponding part of the preceding sentence. Read the sentences to your partner.**

1.

	Shall	we	begin,	ladies and gentlemen?
adjourn vote open the discussion I get started				

2.

	Our research	shows	there's
our study indicates for our new line an excellent market there exists			
	a great potential market		for our products.

3.

	He's	worked out	an	impressive	campaign
exciting proposed scheme come up with profitable					
	for us.				

4.

	We should emphasize the quality			
the excellence stress of the design they the utility				
	of our products.			

5.

	I've	come up with	some	really	great	names.
ideas excellent a few thought of we've						

E. Indicate whether *must* **expresses obligation or probability in each of the following sentences.**

EXAMPLE
I'm sorry, Sir, but they must have gone out for lunch. *Probability.*

1. The younger executives must be preparing something.
2. You must have heard the rumors.
3. You must tell me what is happening.
4. You must think I'm crazy if you expect me to believe that story.
5. We must avoid open conflict between factions.
6. She must be really sick if she stayed home from work.
7. There's something I must tell you.
8. He must be telling his friends everything.

F. Fill in the blanks with *must* **or** *mustn't.*

EXAMPLE
You _*must*_ finish the report before you leave; we're sending it out tonight.

1. You _____ make an effort to understand banking; it's part of your job.
2. You _____ give up smoking; it's bad for you.
3. You _____ believe everything you read in the papers; they sometimes make mistakes.
4. You _____ try not to worry about the office when you are at home; you'll get ulcers if you worry all the time.
5. You _____ worry, Bill; Ron is reliable and can do the job.
6. We _____ spend so much money on advertising; we can't afford it.

G. Discuss the following question.

Choose a product. Imagine that you have to organize an advertising campaign to sell this product. Which of the usual advertising media—newspapers, magazines, trade journals, trade fairs, billboards, television and radio—would be most effective for your campaign?

H. Write a memo to your boss outlining your advertising campaign for the product that you have just discussed.

11 After the Board Meeting

After an exhausting meeting about the advertising campaign, the board has agreed to introduce the new line at the trade fair in Chicago. With promotional packets, ads in trade journals, and an innovative display stand, they hope to have a great initial impact at the fair. Afterwards, the actual selling will be done by the company's team of traveling sales personnel. They will be aided by continued advertising in trade journals. The "homework" done by Bill Roy and his management team has paid off.

Characters: Bill Roy
                   Rod Milton
                   Fred Miller

Scene: Bill's office

Bill: We got what we wanted.

Rod: You got what *you* wanted! But they killed my radio commercial.

Fred: Look, it could have been worse. You might have had Bernie Sutherland on TV, dressed as an astronaut, telling people to buy "Startwister" screwdrivers, or dressed as a cowboy, talking about "Boltwrangler" wrenches.

Bill: Now Fred, that wasn't such a bad idea.

Fred: You're right! Rod's off-key singing would have been even worse.

Rod: Okay, okay. I get the message.

Bill: Now, our next job is to have a word with Anna Vilas, keeper of the purse strings.

Fred: I'd like to see her face when you tell her. She won't be happy about all these extra expenses.

Bill: Oh, she already knows what to expect. I told her I was against the radio and TV spots, but supported the display stands and the campaign at the trade fair.

Fred: Well, Rod. It looks as though you'll have more than enough to keep you busy.

Dialogue Summary

Both Bill Roy and Fred Miller are pleased with the results of the board meeting, although Rod Milton is disappointed because his pet schemes have not been approved. Bill informs Fred that Anna Vilas is prepared for an increased advertising budget. After some friendly teasing, Fred reminds Rod that he will have plenty of work preparing the display stands and the promotional packets for the trade fair.

Exercises

A. Answer these questions about the conversation.

1. Was Bill Roy satisfied with the results of the board meeting?
2. What might have happened if Mr. Sutherland had gotten what he wanted?
3. How will Anna Vilas feel about the advertising campaign expenses?
4. What will keep Rod Milton busy?

B. Select the alternative which best describes what happens in the conversation.

1. Fred, Bill, and Rod are   a. having an informal discussion.
     b. still in the board room.
     c. watching a TV program.

2. Rod is upset because the board   a. didn't like his singing.
     b. killed someone.
     c. rejected his radio commercial.

3. Fred thinks that Mr. Sutherland would be   a. excellent on TV.
     b. against TV advertising:
     c. terrible on TV.

4. Fred is   a. being thoughtful   when he talks about Rod's singing.
     b. being helpful
     c. teasing

5. Anna Vilas is   a. prepared for   the board's decision.
     b. unprepared for
     c. indifferent to

6. Fred knows Rod is going to be   a. useless.
     b. very busy.
     c. singing a lot.

C. Fill in the blanks using the most appropriate word from the right-hand column.

1. We _____ what we wanted.
2. It _____ have been worse.
3. The new line was _____ at the fair.
4. The salespeople will be _____ by ads.

    a. could
    b. introduced
    c. aided
    d. got

5. Our next job is to have a _____ with Anna.
6. Did you design the promotional _____ ?
7. It wasn't a bad _____ .
8. We'll have a great initial _____ .

    a. idea
    b. impact
    c. word
    d. packets

9. The team's work has paid _____ .
10. We'll introduce the line _____ the fair.
11. I saw him _____ TV.
12. I was _____ the idea.

    a. on
    b. against
    c. off
    d. at

13. It was an _____ meeting.
14. The _____ selling is done by sales personnel.
15. We'll have a _____ stand.
16. They have a team of _____ sales personnel.

    a. traveling
    b. display
    c. actual
    d. exhausting

17. It wasn't _____ a bad idea.
18. You'll have more than _____ to keep you busy.
19. She _____ knows what to expect.
20. There will be _____ of work.

    a. already
    b. plenty
    c. such
    d. enough

D. Work in pairs. Make new sentences by using the word or phrase from the left column in place of the corresponding part of the preceding sentence. If the subject changes, make the appropriate changes in the rest of the sentence. Read the sentences to your partner.

1.

	It could have been worse.
better might more difficult should less expensive	

2.

	She won't be happy about the extra expenses.
work couldn't unexpected delays budget cuts	

3.

	She knows what to expect.
to say she's decided they to do discussed	

4.

	I told him I was against the TV spot.
her radio for commercial voted	

5.

	You'll have more than enough to keep you busy.
going plenty there's occupied hardly anything	

E. Complete the sentences with *must have, may have,* or *couldn't have.*

EXAMPLE
She _couldn't have_ taken the car—it's still in the garage.

1. He _____ been very short of money if he was able to buy a new car.
2. You _____ been worn out after playing tennis all morning.
3. She _____ been furious when she found out that someone had stolen her car.
4. We decided to ask the boss again because we thought that he _____ changed his mind.
5. He _____ been very serious about the job if he didn't even fill out an application.
6. I really don't know why Janet didn't answer her phone last night. She _____ gone to bed early, or she _____ gone for a walk.

F. Choose the correct alternative.

EXAMPLE
It   a. must have been   late when he arrived.
      b. had to be
It must have been late when he arrived. (a)

1. When it started to snow we   a. must have driven   carefully.
                             b. had to drive

2. She   a. must have been   worth a fortune when she died.
      b. had to be

3. The company regulations said he   a. must have retired   at 65.
                                 b. had to retire

4. It   a. must have rained   during the night.
      b. had to rain

5. The police officer said they   a. must have gone   to court.
                             b. had to go

6. They   a. must have done   something wrong.
      b. had to do

G. Act out the following situation with a partner. One partner will take Role 1 and the other will take Role 2.

1. You're John Anderson, one of Allgood's sales personnel. You've always worked in the East in a territory right near your home. Now you're going to have to travel and spend a great deal of time on the West Coast. You know your wife won't be happy about your being away so much. You complain to Emil Khan, another sales representative. You think that Allgood should have chosen someone else for this.

2. You're Emil Khan. Although John is very upset, you know working in the West isn't so bad. The West has some beautiful cities and is a good territory. He probably could get good commissions. Convince him that it could have been worse. Allgood might have sent him to the Midwest, where the weather is very severe. Remind him also that his wife can travel and would probably love to visit places like San Francisco. He should be glad that he doesn't have the same problem as Karen Goodrich, another sales representative, whose husband works on weekends and therefore can't travel at all.

H. Write the text of Bernie Sutherland's TV commercial. You may advertise either "Startwister" screwdrivers or "Boltwrangler" wrenches.

12 Patents

Allgood is about to introduce its new screwdriver at the trade fair. Bill receives a letter from Steven Heller, patent attorney for Stopwell Manufacturing, Inc. Apparently Stopwell has gotten wind of Allgood's plans, and has taken out the patent rights on this particular design of screwdriver before the Allgood patent could be accepted. However, Judy Lalonde, a lawyer who represents Allgood, has found out from their research and development department that the new design isn't really as new as the designers claim. They have merely made slight improvements on an old design which was patented by Allgood years before.

Characters: Bill Roy

Steven Heller, patent attorney for Stopwell
Manufacturing, Inc.

Scene: Bill's office

Bill: It appears that both our companies have come up
with similar ideas at about the same time, and
quite independently of each other.

Mr. Heller: But with one slight qualification. Unfortunately
for you and your plans for the fair, Mr. Roy,
Stopwell was a little ahead of your company.

Bill:	I'm sorry, Mr. Heller, but I don't think that's quite correct. You are not in possession of all the facts.
Mr. Heller:	I beg your pardon?
Bill:	You see, our lawyer has discovered some very interesting material. She's a very thorough person.
Mr. Heller:	I'm sure she is. And exactly what has she discovered?
Bill:	This. *(He hands drawings to Mr. Heller.)* It's a design for a screwdriver which was patented by Allgood years ago. You'll agree it was very advanced for its time.
Mr. Heller:	Well, yes.
Bill:	You've noted the similarities between your company's new screwdriver and ours. Now you can also see that our new screwdriver is actually a slightly improved version of this particular design.
Mr. Heller:	Please continue, Mr. Roy.
Bill:	And since the patent on this design precedes the one on yours by a number of years, we will continue with our plans for the trade fair.
Mr. Heller:	I admit that this seems to change the situation, but my company's experts will still have to study these drawings before we reach any conclusions.

Dialogue Summary

Bill Roy is holding the "trump card" when Mr. Heller, Stopwell's patent attorney, comes to see him. Bill explains that Allgood was the first to patent the design and therefore will present its new line at the trade fair as planned.

Exercises

A. Answer these questions about the conversation.

1. Why was Bill holding the "trump card" at this meeting?
2. When was this design patented by Allgood?
3. What role had Allgood's designers played in the development of their "new" design?

B. Select the alternative which best describes what happens in the conversation.

1. Stopwell had   a. already patented   a design similar to Allgood's.
                       b. never patented
                       c. been about to patent

2. Judy Lalonde   a. found out the truth.
                       b. found the new design.
                       c. improved the new design.

3. Allgood's designers hadn't really   a. claimed the design was new.
                                         b. improved the design at all.
                                         c. come up with a completely new design.

4. a. Stopwell   was the first to patent the design.
    b. The patent attorney
    c. Allgood

5. Bill knew that Allgood had   a. something to fear from   Stopwell.
                              b. nothing to fear from
                              c. a real problem with

6. Mr. Heller didn't   a. have all the facts.
                            b. note the similarities between the two
                               screwdrivers.
                            c. look at the drawings.

C. Fill in the blanks using the most appropriate word from the right-hand column.

1. They were about to _____ their design.   a. lawyer
2. They got _____ of Allgood's plans.   b. patent
3. Mrs. Lalonde is a _____ .   c. wind
4. The _____ has been accepted.   d. introduce

5. There's only one _____ qualification.   a. patent
6. Mr. Heller is a _____ attorney.   b. similar
7. She's a very _____ person.   c. slight
8. Our ideas are _____ to theirs.   d. thorough

9. What _____ has she discovered?   a. ahead
10. The designers had _____ made slight improvements.   b. quite
11. Stopwell was a little _____ of Allgood.   c. exactly
12. That's not _____ correct.   d. merely

13. The companies came _____ with the same ideas.   a. out
14. Stopwell had taken _____ patent rights.   b. with
15. We'll continue _____ our plans.   c. about
16. It happened at _____ the same time.   d. up

17. The design was _____ for its time.   a. reached
18. We haven't _____ a conclusion yet.   b. handed
19. The design had been _____ by Allgood.   c. advanced
20. Bill _____ the drawings to Mr. Heller.   d. patented

D. Work in pairs. Make new sentences by using the word or phrase from the left column in place of the corresponding part of the preceding sentence. If the subject changes, make the appropriate changes in the rest of the sentence. Read the sentences to your partner.

1.

	I'm sorry, but I don't think that's quite correct.
accurate completely not convinced his reasoning positive	

2.

	Our lawyer has discovered some interesting material.
my secretary documents found important	

3.

	It's a design which was patented years ago.
developed some time approved invention last year	

4.

	We'll continue with our plans for the exhibition.
trade fair go on future they'll projects	

5.

designs engineers change plans must	My company's experts will have to study these drawings.

E. Fill in the blanks with *up* **or** *down*.

EXAMPLE
Although there was great excitement when the stolen paintings turned __up__ in a subway station, it all died __down__ in less than a week.

1. When you pick _____ a book like that, it's hard to put it _____ .
2. He slowed _____ so that the others could catch _____ .
3. She asked her secretary to hurry _____ and take _____ the minutes.
4. They made _____ their minds to cut _____ on gasoline, when the price went _____ again.
5. She took _____ judo, but gave it _____ after a month.
6. When I called him _____ he promised me the job; but he let me _____ .

F. Fill in the blanks with *back* **or** *away*.

EXAMPLE
The office isn't far __away__ ; please go __back__ there and get my notes.

1. They went _____ for a vacation and came _____ tanned and rested.
2. The boat turned _____ because of bad weather.
3. She turned her head _____ because she couldn't stand the sight of blood.
4. When they moved to Hawaii, they gave _____ their winter clothes and gave _____ all the books they had borrowed.
5. We couldn't get any closer because we were held _____ by a police blockade.
6. Are the Millers _____ from vacation yet?
7. How many days this week have you been _____ from the office?

G. Act out the following situation with a partner. One partner will take Role 1 and the other will take Role 2.

1. You're a very reputable patent attorney. You're extremely thorough in your research. You're also very careful about who you represent. You're interviewing a client who wants you to write the patent for his or her new invention. Before you agree to do this you want to know about the person, how long he or she has been working on this invention, where the work has been done (at home or in the laboratory of some company) and, of course, what the invention is and what makes it different from other similar articles.

2. You have just invented an ingenious article and you want this particular lawyer to represent you and to write out the patent for your invention. Describe your invention (a rocking chair that rocks sideways as well as front and back, or a mechanical back scratcher, or an electrical ball point pen, or a pickpocket proof purse or wallet for example) and explain why it is revolutionary in design. Also answer other questions about how you came up with the invention.

H. Write a 150-word article on the following question.

Why is a research and development department vital to the future of any manufacturing company?

13 Sales: Problems and Perspectives

Janet Casella has begun her new job as assistant marketing manager in Fred Miller's department. Sales are down and she wants to make a report on all possible factors. She's about to meet with Andy Johnson, one of Allgood's oldest and most trusted sales representatives.

Characters: Janet Casella

Andy Johnson, sales representative

Scene: Janet's office

Janet: It's good to see you, Andy. Please sit down.

Andy: Thank you. Is there something in particular you want to discuss?

Janet: Yes. How long have you been working in your present territory?

Andy: Quite a few years now . . . five to be exact.

Janet: I thought you were very familiar with the area. But I see your sales are also down this quarter. Any problems?

Andy: Well, last quarter was an exceptionally good one.

Janet: But what about this quarter? I'd like to see you win the sales award again.

Andy: I'd like to win it too. But, actually, the market is much slower now. I think sales have gone down because we raised our prices two months ago.

Janet: You've got a point. Also, maybe our market is too limited. What do you think?

Andy: I agree. Right now our products are aimed at a special market. We're making tools almost exclusively for skilled craftsmen or for very sophisticated amateurs.

Janet: If we introduced a lower quality product at a cheaper price, do you think we would have a larger market?

Andy: I don't have too much faith in the idea that "the cheaper they are, the more they sell." But it's something to think about. And here's something else: the efficiency of our shipping department.

Janet: Why do you say that?

Andy: On my way here, I dropped in at Johnson's Hardware to check on an order. I was sent straight to the boss's office and he let me have it.

Janet: What was the trouble?

Andy: First of all, the order was delivered three weeks late. The chisels we sent were the wrong size, and finally, part of the shipment was damaged. It hadn't been packed properly.

Janet: That's pretty poor service. I'll speak to Fred about it.

Andy: Thanks. It would be a lot easier for us if the shipping department filled the orders correctly and sent them out on time.

Dialogue Summary

Andy Johnson's sales are down and Janet asks him why. They discuss causes and possible solutions. Andy is upset because he has just visited a dissatisfied customer and he thinks the shipping department isn't doing its job properly.

Exercises

A. Answer these questions about the conversation.

1. What reason does Andy Johnson give at first for reduced sales?
2. What is Andy's attitude towards a lower quality product?
3. What happened when Andy dropped in at Johnson's Hardware?
4. What improvements would Andy like to see at Allgood?

B. Select the alternative which best describes what happens in the conversation.

1. Andy Johnson is talking with the   a. marketing manager.
   b. assistant marketing manager.
   c. production manager.

2. Andy's sales are   a. up.
   b. average.
   c. down.

3. Sales have gone down because the   a. prices went up.
   b. advertising budget is too limited.
   c. sales representatives aren't working hard.

4. Allgood makes tools for   a. skilled craftsmen.
   b. American supermarkets.
   c. inexperienced amateurs.

5. The boss at Johnson's Hardware was   a. friendly   with Andy.
   b. angry
   c. happy

6. The order was   a. three days   late.
   b. three weeks
   c. three months

C. Fill in the blanks using the most appropriate word from the right-hand column.

1. Last quarter was an _____ good one.   a. straight
2. That's _____ poor service.   b. again
3. I was sent _____ to his office.   c. exceptionally
4. He'd like to win the sales award _____.   d. pretty

5. Your sales are _____ this quarter.   a. on
6. It's something to think _____.   b. at
7. Our products are aimed _____ a special market.   c. down
8. She checked _____ an order.   d. about

94

9. He _____ me have it.
10. The order was _____ three weeks late.
11. You've _____ a point.
12. We _____ our prices last month.

a. delivered
b. got
c. let
d. raised

13. Here's something _____ .
14. Our market is _____ limited.
15. I don't have _____ faith in it.
16. It'd be a _____ easier if they were careful.

a. too
b. lot
c. else
d. much

17. We make tools for _____ craftsmen.
18. This is a _____ quality product.
19. Do you want anything in _____ ?
20. Andy is _____ with the area.

a. particular
b. familiar
c. lower
d. skilled

D. Work in pairs. Make new sentences by using the word or phrase from the left column in place of the corresponding part of the preceding sentence. If the subject changes, make the appropriate changes in the rest of the sentence. Read the sentences to your partner.

1.

	How long have you been working in your present territory?
selling this since when she area	

2.

	I see your sales are down this quarter.
up noticed were last week	

95

3.

	Our market is too limited.
much too product expensive screwdrivers cheap	

4.

	We're making equipment for skilled craftsmen.
professionals manufacturing tools selling instruments	

5.

	I dropped in at Johnson's Hardware to check
a bill to see about a hardware store stopped Andy	
	on an order.

E. Fill in the blanks with *much* **or** *many.*

EXAMPLE
How _much_ of your campaign is already prepared?

1. How _____ will it change the company's image?
2. How _____ interest will be charged on the loan?
3. How _____ of the usual media will we make use of?
4. How _____ people buy directly from the factory?
5. How _____ items are on display?

F. Insert *too much* **or** *too* **in each sentence.**

EXAMPLE
It's expensive.
It's too expensive.

1. We're busy as it is.
2. You've got confidence.
3. The company is small.
4. They're giving us competition.
5. It's difficult to get him to change his mind.

G. Complete these sentences by adding a negative or affirmative tag question such as, *weren't they?; hadn't he?; could you?; wouldn't it?* **and so forth.**

EXAMPLE
The men conducting the survey were there, _weren't they ?_

1. Bill had been on a trip out west, _____ ?
2. I've always been honest with you, _____ ?
3. That would be one of the men doing the survey, _____ ?
4. You couldn't call me back later, _____ ?
5. He shouldn't have called Bill back, _____ ?
6. Nobody told the workmen about the survey, _____ ?
7. Nothing's gone wrong, _____ ?

97

H. Act out the following situation with a partner. One partner will take Role 1 and the other will take Role 2.

1. You're Mr. Mandell, an old and trusted customer. Allgood promised to ship toolboxes which you planned to sell as a Christmas special. It's now December 15th and the goods haven't arrived yet. You're furious because you lost a lot of potential sales (they were a very popular item last Christmas season). There isn't enough time now to sell a complete shipment even if it arrives tomorrow. You don't want to get stuck with a dozen or more leftover Christmas gift toolboxes. You're calling Allgood to cancel your order.

2. You're an Allgood representative. Shipments of the Christmas special toolboxes were delayed: there were a number of last minute improvements in the design which delayed the production of the *new* toolboxes. However, everyone at Allgood thinks the delay was worthwhile: customers are just beginning to receive their shipments and already they're calling to reorder because the toolboxes are a very hot item and sell out in one day. Try to calm Mr. Mandell. Promise that he'll receive his shipment the day after tomorrow.

I. Do you believe that amateurs prefer to use inexpensive tools of inferior quality for their hobbies? Explain your answer in 150 words.

14 Industrial Accident

While Janet Casella is trying to clear up problems in the sales department, Jim Jackson is having problems in personnel. There has been an accident in the shop, and a worker has injured an eye. Jim is meeting with the shop supervisor to find out exactly what happened.

Characters: Jim Jackson, personnel manager

Ken Ling, shop supervisor

Scene: Jim's office

Jim: Sit down, Ken. It was an unfortunate accident and I know you feel bad about it.

Ken: I sure do. Getting injured in the eye is no joke.

Jim: Well, we'll keep our fingers crossed. *(He pauses.)* I hope it wasn't a problem with the machinery.

Ken: No. Ed was careless. He wasn't wearing his goggles.

Jim: Does he do that a lot?

Ken: Sometimes, I guess. But he's been working here for over a year. He should know the safety regulations by now.

Jim: You've made sure of that?

Ken: Of course. They're posted everywhere and reviewed every so often in our shop meetings. Of course the workers don't like the goggles very much.

Jim: Why is that?

Ken: They claim that they're very uncomfortable, and they're hard to see through. Sometimes they take them off because they're having trouble seeing the machinery.

Jim: Where were you at the time of the accident?

Ken: I was on the delivery ramp.

Jim: Do you know whether Ed put his goggles on and then took them off or didn't put them on at all?

Ken: I told you, didn't I? I wasn't there. I was on the ramp.

Jim: Don't misunderstand me, Ken. I just want to get the facts straight. *(He pauses.)* I guess we'll have to order better goggles for the workers. They cost a little more, but it's probably worth the investment.

Ken: I agree. In fact, I think we should take another look at *all* the protective clothing the workers wear.

Dialogue Summary

Jim Jackson, the personnel manager, and Ken Ling, the shop supervisor, are discussing an accident that has just taken place in the shop. Ken doesn't know why the employee wasn't wearing his protective goggles. Jim sees that the accident is partly due to personal carelessness. But he also sees that the company may be at fault for not having chosen safer, more comfortable goggles.

Exercises

A. Answer these questions about the conversation.

1. How did the worker get injured?
2. Why don't the workers follow the regulation on goggles?
3. Where was the shop supervisor when the accident took place?
4. Why is Jim asking Ken such detailed questions?
5. How is the company going to deal with the problem?

B. Select the alternative which best describes what happens in the conversation.

1. There has been   a. a fire   in the plant.
                     b. a fight
                     c. an accident

2. Jim is interviewing the   a. shop supervisor.
                              b. injured man.
                              c. safety officer.

3. The injured man   a. didn't have any   safety goggles.
                     b. was wearing
                     c. wasn't wearing

4. The workers don't like the goggles because   a. they're comfortable.
                                                   b. they're hard to see through.
                                                   c. they're required.

5. Jim is trying to   a. find out the facts.
                       b. blame Ken for the accident.
                       c. prove that someone was responsible.

6. Jim and Ken agree that   a. the safety regulations are inadequate.
                            b. better goggles would be a good
                               investment.
                            c. the accident was completely due to
                               personal carelessness.

C. Fill in the blanks using the most appropriate word from the right-hand column.

1. We'll have to keep our _____ crossed.
2. The _____ are posted everywhere.
3. He forgot to put on his _____ .
4. Let's get the _____ straight.

a. regulations
b. facts
c. fingers
d. goggles

5. He's been working here _____ over a year.
6. Getting injured _____ the eye is no joke.
7. He should know them _____ now.
8. He didn't put them on _____ all.

a. in
b. by
c. at
d. for

9. Getting _____ is no joke.
10. They're _____ every so often.
11. We've _____ sure of it.
12. The accident was _____ to carelessness.

a. due
b. made
c. injured
d. reviewed

13. They have _____ seeing through the goggles.
14. The _____ took place in the shop.
15. The company may be at _____ .
16. An eye injury is no _____ .

a. fault
b. joke
c. trouble
d. accident

17. It was an _____ accident.
18. He wore the proper _____ clothing.
19. He was just _____ .
20. I was on the _____ ramp at the time.

a. careless
b. protective
c. delivery
d. unfortunate

102

D. Work in pairs. Make new sentences by using the word or phrase from the left column in place of the corresponding part of the preceding sentence. If the subject changes, make the appropriate changes in the rest of the sentence. Read the sentences to your partner.

1.

	He's been working here for over a year.
month in this town living they in New York	

2.

	He should know the safety regulations by now.
his responsibilities be aware of obligations have fulfilled before	

3.

	They're having trouble seeing the machinery.
using equipment difficulty the workers problems	

4.

	Where were you at the time of the accident?
they during proceedings he after	

5.

	I just want to get the facts straight.
wanted only details tried they	

E. Add *very much* to the following sentences.

EXAMPLE
He doesn't enjoy dining out.
He doesn't enjoy dining out very much.

1. He doesn't want to succeed.
2. They don't emphasize safety regulations.
3. We don't like TV commercials.
4. She doesn't enjoy trade fairs.
5. Does it matter if they don't wear the goggles?

F. Make the following sentences affirmative. Note that *much* in the negative becomes *a lot* in the affirmative.

EXAMPLE
He hasn't written much today.
He's written a lot today.

1. The company's image hasn't changed much over the last few years.
2. He won't get much out of it.
3. I didn't like the ads we saw very much.
4. It won't cost very much.
5. He doesn't sell much on Fridays.
6. There isn't much to be said for the new system.

G. Act out the following situation with a partner. One partner will take Role 1 and the other will take Role 2.

1. You're a shop supervisor. One of your employees refuses to wear protective gloves when he or she washes the acid tank. This is a very dangerous job. You know two people who had accidents while doing this and injured their hands permanently. The employee is a very skilled worker and performs many important tasks. Try to persuade the employee to wear the gloves.

2. You're the employee. You don't like to wear these particular rubber gloves because they're too thick and heavy and you can't feel what you're doing. Also their surface is slippery and you can't hold the scrub brush. The gloves make your hands perspire even when you use talcum powder. You can't do a good job when you wear the gloves, so you refuse to wear them.

H. Write a letter to the editor of the newspaper suggesting ways to prevent traffic accidents in your town.

15 Stolen Money

While Jim Jackson is dealing with the consequences of the accident, Pat Phillips, the assistant comptroller, has just rushed to Anna Vilas's office with a different emergency.

Characters: Anna Vilas, comptroller

Pat Phillips, assistant comptroller

Scene: Anna's office

Anna: What's the problem, Pat?

Pat: We're out two thousand dollars! We deposited a check for this amount and it's been returned by the bank stamped "No Such Account."

Anna: Get the cashier on the phone. Since when do we have a policy of accepting checks without proper verification?

Pat: I don't think that's the problem. Frankly, I suspect fraud. And furthermore, I think that it's someone right here in the company.

Anna: That's a very serious accusation. You'd better tell me the whole story.

Pat: About a week ago, I noticed we'd made a rather unusual deposit: several large checks and almost no cash.

Anna: That's not very unusual. Occasionally the Retail Department reports only a small amount of cash in the day's receipts.

Pat: I know. That's why I didn't say anything then. But when we got the notice, I went across to the bank to see the manager, and we went through the accounts together. It turns out that the bad check was part of the deposit.

Anna: That doesn't mean it was an inside job.

Pat: Retail says we took in just over two thousand dollars in cash on the day the deposit was made. I think someone here took the cash and substituted a bad check for it.

Anna: I hope you're wrong. In any case, we have to notify Bill immediately, and start a formal investigation. As a matter of fact, we'd better go over to his office right now and talk to him in person.

Dialogue Summary

Pat Phillips informs Anna Vilas that $2,000 is missing from the company's account. She believes it is fraud and tells Anna why. Anna decides to talk to Bill Roy and start a formal investigation.

Conclusion

The formal investigation was stopped almost as soon as it started. It turned out to be a minor case of "white-collar crime." An old and trusted employee found himself in financial straits and had "borrowed" the money, hoping to return it before anyone noticed the loss. He confessed as soon as he found out there was an investigation in progress. Because he was able to make full restitution of the money almost immediately, Allgood merely dismissed him and didn't press charges.

Exercises

A. Answer these questions about the conversation.

1. Why has Pat come to see Anna?
2. Why does Anna blame the cashier at first?
3. Why does Pat think it is an inside job?

B. Select the alternative which best describes what happens in the conversation.

1. Anna Vilas manages Allgood's   a. bank.
                                               b. filing system.
                                             c. finances.

2. A $2,000 check has been   a. stamped   by Allgood's bank.
                                           b. returned
                                           c. cashed

3. Allgood's cashier should never accept checks without
    a. a formal investigation.
    b. notification.
    c. proper verification.

4. Pat Phillips tells Anna   a. a funny story.
                              b. the whole story of the apparent theft.
                              c. about Allgood's new checking policy.

5. a. Pat   thinks it was an inside job.
    b. Anna
    c. The bank manager

6. It will be necessary for Allgood to have a formal   a. investigator.
                                                        b. reception.
                                                        c. investigation.

C. Fill in the blanks using the most appropriate word from the right-hand column.

1. Accept checks only with proper _____ .   a. amount
2. Your _____ is very serious.   b. verification
3. There's a small _____ of cash.   c. accusation
4. We deposited hardly any _____ .   d. cash

5. It turned _____ to be a bad check.   a. by
6. $2,000 is missing _____ the account.   b. in
7. It was returned _____ the bank.   c. from
8. There's no cash _____ today's receipts.   d. out

9. It wasn't an _____ deposit.   a. whole
10. Tell me the _____ story.   b. inside
11. This is an _____ job.   c. unusual
12. We must have a _____ investigation.   d. formal

13. We went _____ the accounts.   a. on
14. We took in _____ $2,000.   b. out
15. We're _____ $3,500.   c. through
16. The cashier is _____ the phone.   d. over

17. Pat _____ fraud.   a. developed
18. Somebody _____ a bad check for the cash.   b. notified
19. Have we _____ a new policy?   c. substituted
20. Anna _____ Bill immediately.   d. suspected

D. Work in pairs. Make new sentences by using the word or phrase from the left column in place of the corresponding part of the preceding sentence. If the subject changes, make the appropriate changes in the rest of the sentence. Read the sentences to your partner.

1.

	Since when do we have a policy of accepting checks?
rejecting you customers being rude to does he	

2.

	You'd better tell me the whole story.
truth them details she had to	

3.

	That doesn't mean it was an inside job.
prove bad deal fraudulent scheme	

4.

	I think that someone here took the cash.
somebody money suspect check substituted	

5.

	We have to notify Bill immediately.
had better at once him must tell	

E. For each sentence select the two prepositions that can be used. Choose from: *through, over,* **and** *across.*

EXAMPLE
Did you go __*over/through*__ the accounts?

1. We walked _____ the George Washington Bridge.
2. They went back to the office and looked _____ the drawings.
3. We were frightened when we flew _____ the Pacific.
4. The man at the next table leaned _____ and asked me to pass the salt.
5. We went _____ all the procedures very carefully.
6. We travelled _____ Europe by train.

F. Put the verbs in parentheses into either the simple present tense or the *going to* **future tense.**

EXAMPLE
We usually (place) our orders at the beginning of the week, but I think we (change) this procedure.
We usually *place* our orders at the beginning of the week, but I think we're *going to change* this procedure.

1. When I (leave) on Fridays I (leave) my worries behind me.
2. I always (plan) something special for Friday evenings.
3. Take this Friday for example: I (meet) a few of my friends after work.
4. We (have) a few drinks, Chinese food, and then we (go) to the movies.
5. There (be) a sneak preview of a new film this Friday, but I (can not) remember the name.

G. Act out the following situation with a partner. One partner will take Role 1 and the other will take Role 2.

1. You're a shop assistant and a customer is accusing you of giving him or her the wrong change. You think the customer gave you a ten-dollar bill. The customer claims it was a twenty-dollar bill. This is a candy store where most of the items cost less than one dollar. Customers usually pay with change or one-dollar or five-dollar bills. You're sure you would have noticed a twenty because they're so unusual. There's a twenty in the cash box, but you're pretty sure that a customer gave it to you earlier.

2. You're the customer. You know you gave the assistant a twenty-dollar bill. You're very careful about money: you put two twenty-dollar bills in your wallet before you left your house. This is the first place you've stopped and the first purchase that you've made. You have only one twenty left. You want the correct change.

H. Pretend that you are Anna Vilas. Write a memo to Bill Roy explaining that two thousand dollars is missing and how you think it happened.

4. Bill plans to   a. practice his golf.
                  b. find another job.
                  c. become a government adviser.

5. Bill also wants to visit   a. Singapore.
                          b. India.
                          c. Paris.

6. Fred thinks that   a. the company will be managed better.
                 b. the company will have problems.
                 c. things won't be the same without Bill.

C. Fill in the blanks using the most appropriate word from the right-hand column.

1. The shipment is long _____ .   a. last
2. Friday's the _____ day of the business week.   b. easy
3. They're making a _____ tour of India.   c. overdue
4. Lowering my golf handicap is no _____ job.   d. leisurely

5. We _____ to visit my son.   a. spend
6. Bill is not going to _____ away.   b. second
7. I'll _____ the motion.   c. intend
8. We'll _____ some time in Bali.   d. fade

9. The country is having a _____ .   a. hand
10. This is a _____ of my speech.   b. handicap
11. She had a _____ in the menu planning.   c. preview
12. His golf _____ is in the single figures.   d. recession

13. He's sad to be _____ .   a. taking
14. What are you _____ at the banquet?   b. preparing
15. I'm pleased you're _____ over my job.   c. leaving
16. He's _____ for the formal presentation.   d. serving

D. Work in pairs. Make new sentences by using the word or phrase from the left column in place of the corresponding part of the preceding sentence. If the subject changes, make the appropriate changes in the rest of the sentence. Read the sentences to your partner.

1.

	My wife and I are hoping to leave
our representatives a few weeks return after expect	
	in about a month.

2.

	I've always been fascinated by the East.
oriental rugs interested in traveling never we	

3.

	I intend to spend some time in Bali.
plan a few weeks the West stay we'd like	

4.

	I'll think of you the next time there's a recession.
call an overdue shipment every time we have strike	

5.

	I must say I'm pleased you're taking over.
admit replacing me delighted have to relieved	

E. Fill in the blanks with an appropriate preposition.

EXAMPLE
Please show them _to_ the conference room.

1. Is your factory _____ the bus route?
2. I heard _____ it by accident.
3. Did she show any interest _____ the project?
4. Have they referred _____ your project?
5. I'm afraid that they laughed _____ my idea.
6. I spoke _____ him _____ the phone last night.
7. When she's silent, I know she's thinking _____ something.

F. Explain why the following sentences are incorrect and amusing. Then rewrite them correctly.

EXAMPLE
The lady bought the painting in the polka dot dress.
The position of the modifying phrase, *in the polka dot dress,* is incorrect. The phrase modifies *lady,* not *painting,* and should be placed after the word it modifies. *The lady in the polka dot dress bought the painting.*

183

1. Wanted: man to drive truck with references.
2. The businessman was hit by a bus on a motor scooter.
3. Two hunters were attacked by some tigers on safari.
4. The woman ordered the table in the blue suit with mahogany legs.
5. The customer ordered a hamburger and french fries with a beard.

G. Act out the following situation with a partner. One partner will take Role 1 and the other will take Role 2.

1. It is your last day at your present job (or at school). Explain your future plans to your friend.

2. It is your last day, too. Tell your friend of your plans for the coming year.

H. Discuss the following topic.

What do you think the retirement age should be in your country? Should all people be required to retire at the same age? Should the retirement age be the same for men and women? Is it a waste of talent and experience to expect older people to retire even though they are perfectly capable of fulfilling their duties? Consider the problem of older people preventing younger ones from holding important positions. Also consider the effect on the person who is retiring.

I. Write Bill Roy's farewell speech.

ANSWER KEY

1 BILL ROY'S WORKING DAY

A. Suggested Answers

1. Bill Roy is the general manager of Allgood Engineering.
2. He has too many appointments and never has a moment to himself.
3. He doesn't. He asks Janet to deal with Mr. Sutherland.
4. No, he doesn't.
5. There's trouble in the shop.

B.
1. c	5. a
2. b	6. a
3. b	7. b
4. b	8. c

C.
1. d	5. d	9. d	13. b	17. b
2. c	6. a	10. b	14. c	18. a
3. a	7. b	11. c	15. d	19. d
4. b	8. c	12. a	16. a	20. c

D. 1. He says he has to see you tomorrow.
He says he wants to see you tomorrow.
He says he wants to discuss it with you tomorrow.
He says he wants to discuss it with us tomorrow.
He says he wants to discuss it with us right away.

2. Have the reports arrived from the patent bureau?
   Have the reports arrived from the main office?
   Have the statements arrived from the main office?
   Have the statements arrived from the bank?
   Haven't the statements arrived from the bank?

3. The shop steward is here.
   The shop steward was here.
   The shop steward was in Detroit.
   The shop mechanic was in Detroit.
   The shop mechanic has been in Detroit.

4. I'll go and pick up your mail now.
   I'll go and pick up your mail right away.
   I'll go and send your mail right away.
   I'll go and send your report right away.
   I'll go and find your report right away.

E. Suggested Answers

1. When is Mr. Block's appointment?
2. What is on Bill's desk?
3. Which reports were sent to Mrs. Lalonde?
4. Whose appointment is at ten?
5. Why does Mr. Ling want to see Bill?

F.
1. buy
2. have or receive
3. earn
4. find
5. wins

2 PERSONNEL PROBLEMS

A. Suggested Answers

1. Bill is referring to the news of Mike Edwards's resignation.
2. He's found a better job with more money.
3. He thinks she will be good in the marketing department.
4. Bill will be losing the best assistant he has ever had.
5. They are advertising for an administrative assistant to a senior executive.

B. 1. a   5. b
     2. b   6. c
     3. c   7. b
     4. b   8. c

C. 1. b   5. d   9. c   13. c   17. c
     2. d   6. c   10. d   14. a   18. d
     3. a   7. b   11. b   15. d   19. a
     4. c   8. a   12. a   16. b   20. b

D. 1. I'm usually too busy to listen to gossip.
     I'm usually too busy to listen to complaints.
     I'm usually too tired to listen to complaints.
     He's usually too tired to listen to complaints.
     He's usually too irritated to listen to complaints.

     2. Do you have anybody in mind to replace her?
     Do you have anybody in mind to train her?
     Does he have anybody in mind to train her?
     Does he have somebody in mind to train her?
     Does he have somebody in mind to work with her?

     3. I'll be losing the best secretary I've ever had.
     I'll be losing the most efficient secretary I've ever had.
     I'll be losing the most efficient secretary I've ever known.
     I'll be losing the most efficient representative I've ever known.
     I'll be losing the worst representative I've ever known.

     4. You'll find a new marketing manager.
     He'll find a new marketing manager.
     He'll hire a new marketing manager.
     He'll hire a new receptionist.
     He'll hire a good receptionist.

     5. The vacancy must be filled immediately.
     The vacancy must be filled right away.
     The position must be filled right away.
     The position should be filled right away.
     The position should be filled now.

E. 1. Bill has just avoided a strike.
     2. Have you heard the news yet?
     3. I've never seen that report.
     4. She's the best assistant I've ever had.
     5. Bill has already read the mail.

F. 1. since
    2. for
    3. for
    4. since
    5. for

3 AN INTERVIEW

A. Suggested Answers

1. Bill is reading the sports section of the *New York Times*.
2. Bill complains that, because his assistant moves his papers, he can never find what he needs.
3. Yes, she has.
4. He talks about his golf lessons.

B. 1. b   5. c
    2. b   6. a
    3. c   7. b
    4. a   8. c

C. 1. b   5. c   9. c   13. b
    2. a   6. a   10. d   14. d
    3. c   7. b   11. b   15. a
    4. d   8. d   12. a   16. c

D. 1. Bring in Ms. Smollar's résumé, please.
    Find Ms. Smollar's résumé, please.
    Find Mr. Smith's résumé, please.
    Find Mr. Smith's application, please.
    Give me Mr. Smith's application, please.

2. I'm sure you have a lot to think about.
    I realize you have a lot to think about.
    I realize you have a lot to worry about.
    I realize you have too much to worry about.
    I realize you have too much to do.

3. I've looked over your reports.
    I've checked your reports.
    They've checked your reports.
    They've checked his reports.
    They've checked his statistics.

4. You seem to have just the sort of background we need.
   You appear to have just the sort of background we need.
   You appear to have just the kind of background we need.
   You appear to have exactly the kind of background we need.
   You appear to have exactly the kind of background we want.

5. Mr. Clark is about to leave for work.
   I'm about to leave for work.
   I'm about to leave for home.
   I'm about to go home.
   I'm ready to go home.

E. **The immediate past is formed with the present perfect + *just* (i.e., The meeting has just started).**
The immediate future is formed with the present of the verb *to be* + *about to* + the infinitive (i.e., The meeting is about to start).

1. about to
2. just
3. about to

4. just
5. about to

F. **The simple past tense is used when actions are situated in past time. Generally, there is a mention of time in the sentence or in the text to indicate when the action took place (i.e., *yesterday, this morning, last week, at Christmas, on my birthday, two weeks ago,* etc.). The simple past tense is also used with "when" questions in the past. The present perfect is used when actions continue up to the present time or take place at an indefinite time in the past. The time markers for this tense are: *up until now, ever, never, already, not yet, for,* and *since.***

1. The last time I saw him was just after Christmas.
2. His father gave him a tape recorder for his birthday.
3. Do you mean to say you've never been to Washington?
4. What did you say to him when he arrived?
5. I've been afraid of her ever since I heard her arguing with the accountant.
6. We signed the contract last week.
7. Last week we put a new door on the office.
8. When he phoned this morning, he surprised his colleagues.
9. She has written articles for that magazine for the past two years.
10. I never forgave (I've never forgiven) him for what he told my competitors.

4 AFTER THE INTERVIEW

A. Suggested Answers

1. Bill didn't ask her anything.
2. No, she doesn't.
3. Yes, she does, since Margaret sent in an excellent résumé.
4. Bill thinks that Janet's work is good.
5. Janet has been working with him for three years.

B.

1. b	5. c
2. c	6. a
3. b	7. b
4. b	8. c

C.

1. b	5. b	9. d	13. b
2. d	6. c	10. c	14. d
3. a	7. d	11. a	15. c
4. c	8. a	12. b	16. a

D. 1. He didn't really ask me any questions.
He didn't really ask us any questions.
He didn't really ask us a single thing.
He didn't really tell us a single thing.
He didn't really tell us the truth.

2. He seemed more interested in his problems.
He seemed more worried about his problems.
He seemed more worried about his board meeting.
He seemed very worried about his board meeting.
He was very worried about his board meeting.

3. He had wonderful things to say about your work.
They had wonderful things to say about your work.
They had wonderful things to say about your character.
They had terrible things to say about your character.
They had terrible things to say about your friends.

4. Do you think I have a good chance of flying to London?
Are you sure I have a good chance of flying to London?
Are you sure he has a good chance of flying to London?
Are you sure he has a good chance of returning home?
Are you sure he has a good chance of finding a replacement?

5. How long has she been working for him?
   How long has she been working for her?
   How long has she been working with her?
   How long has she been living with her?
   Since when has she been living with her?

E.
1. long
2. far
3. old, tall
4. long, wide, deep
5. old, tall, wide
6. many
7. much
8. long, wide

F.

1. a, b, c	5. b	9. c, d	13. a, b	17. b
2. a, b	6. b, c, d	10. a, b, c	14. a, b, c	18. a, c, d
3. c, d	7. b, c, d	11. a	15. b, c, d	19. a, b, d
4. b	8. a	12. a	16. c	20. c

5 MARGARET'S FIRST DAY

A. Suggested Answers

1. Yes, he did.
2. Yes, Jim has come at a good time since the meeting was just finishing up.
3. Bill introduces Margaret.
4. The people at the meeting are Bill Roy, general manager; Fred Miller, marketing director; Anna Vilas, comptroller; and Rod Milton, advertising manager.

B.

1. c	5. a
2. b	6. c
3. a	7. a
4. c	8. b

C.

1. d	5. c	9. c	13. d
2. c	6. a	10. a	14. a
3. b	7. d	11. d	15. c
4. a	8. b	12. b	16. b

D.
1. May I interrupt your conversation?
   Could I interrupt your conversation?
   Could we interrupt your conversation?
   Could we interrupt your speech?
   Could we listen to your speech?

2. She's prepared to start work.
   They're prepared to start work.
   They aren't prepared to start work.
   They aren't prepared to start the project.
   They aren't prepared to begin the project.

3. She couldn't have come at a better time.
   She couldn't have left at a better time.
   She couldn't have left at a better moment.
   She couldn't have left at a worse moment.
   She couldn't have called at a worse moment.

4. That's very nice of you.
   That was very nice of you.
   That was really nice of you.
   That was really thoughtful of you.
   That was really thoughtful of him.

5. We're happy to have you with us.
   We're happy to have you in the company.
   We're delighted to have you in the company.
   I'm delighted to have you in the company.
   I'm delighted to have them in the company.

E. 1. call, phone   4. if
        2. send   5. executives
        3. make, manufacture

F. *To say* **and** *to tell* **have approximately the same meaning, but they are used in different sentence structures:**
   To say **is followed by:**
   — **direct speech (i.e., He said, "I've heard a lot about you.")**
   — *that* **when used in reported speech (i.e., He said** *that* **he had heard a lot about you.)**
   — **reported speech with** *that* **omitted (i.e., He said he had heard a lot about you.)**
   — *to* + **a person (i.e., That's what she said** *to Bill.)*
   To tell **is followed by:**
   — **a person (i.e., She told** *Jim* **she was ready for work.)**
   — **a noun (i.e., He always told** *the truth.)*

   1. tell   4. said
   2. told   5. said
   3. said, told

G. The past progressive tense shows when an action was taking place and is equivalent to a date. The tense of the main clause in the same sentence must be in the simple past.

Bill: I hope that you had a chance to talk to Ms. Casella while you were waiting to be introduced to the management team.

Margaret: She was showing me around the office when Mr. Jackson came to introduce me to everyone.

Bill: Good. I asked her to do that yesterday while we were making a list of unfinished projects. So now you know something about our office procedures.

Margaret: Actually, not much. While she was explaining things to me, the phone rang, and she had a long conversation with someone. Then, when she began (or was beginning) to tell me a few more things, the door opened and Mr. Jackson came out to get me.

6 WORK EFFICIENCY AT ALLGOOD

A. Suggested Answers

1. He feels that the junior people have had something on their minds.
2. He wants to know what is going to happen at the policy meeting.
3. He wants Bill to tell him the truth.
4. Jim is on the side of the junior executives, but he also supports Bill.
5. He feels that it is not the right time to make changes.

B.

1. c	5. b
2. c	6. a
3. b	7. b
4. c	8. b

C.

1. d	5. c	9. c	13. c	17. a
2. c	6. d	10. a	14. d	18. d
3. a	7. b	11. b	15. a	19. c
4. b	8. a	12. d	16. b	20. b

D. 1. I suspect something's happening.
I think something's happening.
He thinks something's happening.
He thinks something could happen.
He thinks anything could happen.

2. They've had a lot on their minds lately.
   They've had too much on their minds lately.
   They've had too much on their minds recently.
   They've had too much to think about recently.
   They've had too much to think about for some time now.

3. I've heard a couple of rumors.
   I've heard a number of rumors.
   They've heard a number of rumors.
   They've started a number of rumors.
   They've started a number of projects.

4. I feel there's room for improvement.
   She feels there's room for improvement.
   She feels there's a chance for improvement.
   She feels there's a chance for advancement.
   She feels there could be a chance for advancement.

5. It's the wrong time to make any improvements.
   It's the wrong time to authorize any improvements.
   It's the wrong time to authorize those improvements.
   It's the right time to authorize those improvements.
   It was the right time to authorize those improvements.

E. **There is no rule explaining which verbs are followed by the** -ing **form of the verb or the infinitive. Unfortunately, these have to be learned as you go along.**

   1. working
   2. sending
   3. to go
   4. reading

   5. to cancel
   6. to get
   7. to discuss

F. 1. put
   2. taken
   3. take
   4. put

   5. take
   6. put
   7. take

7 THE EFFICIENCY STUDY

A. Suggested Answers

1. No, it wasn't.
2. Anna Vilas is in favor of the study. She feels the company would benefit from it.

3. Sandra Ravel feels that there is no need for an efficiency study and that the workers would be upset by one.

B. 1. b   5. c
    2. c   6. a
    3. c   7. b
    4. b   8. c

C. 1. d   5. c   9. c   13. c   17. b
    2. c   6. d   10. a   14. d   18. c
    3. a   7. a   11. d   15. a   19. d
    4. b   8. b   12. b   16. b   20. a

D. 1. That takes care of most of the items on the agenda.
    That takes care of most of the topics on the agenda.
    That takes care of a few of the topics on the agenda.
    Let's discuss a few of the topics on the agenda.
    Let's discuss a few of the topics in the report.

2. I have some questions about the company's efficiency.
    I have a few questions about the company's efficiency.
    I want to ask a few questions about the company's efficiency.
    I want to ask a few questions about the company's policy.
    They posed a few questions about the company's policy.

3. This is definitely a topic for serious discussion.
    This is certainly a topic for serious discussion.
    This is certainly a topic for thoughtful discussion.
    This is obviously a topic for thoughtful discussion.
    This is obviously a topic for thoughtful debate.

4. That was the result of poor labor relations.
    That was the result of poor staff relations.
    That was due to poor staff relations.
    That was due to poor staff cooperation.
    That was due to excellent staff cooperation.

5. The survey only sparked off the battle.
    The survey merely sparked off the battle.
    The report merely sparked off the battle.
    The report merely added to the battle.
    The report merely added to the problem.

E.
1. some, some
2. any
3. some
4. any
5. some

6. some
7. any
8. some
9. any
10. any

F. *Some* **is used for approximative sentences.** *Any* **is used for questions and negative sentences. Remember that words like** *never* **and** *hardly* **are considered negative markers.**

1. nothing
2. something
3. anywhere
4. somewhere

5. anything
6. somebody
7. anybody

8 THE STUDY CREATES A PROBLEM

A. Suggested Answers

1. Ken Ling has come to tell Bill Roy that the workers don't like the survey.
2. He's Art Shafer, the head of the team of consultants.
3. Yes, he was.
4. No, he hasn't.
5. The workers are ready to walk off the job.
6. The study includes valuable suggestions for improving production.

B.
1. c
2. b
3. c
4. c

5. c
6. a
7. c

C.
1. b
2. c
3. d
4. a

5. c
6. d
7. a
8. b

9. c
10. d
11. a
12. b

13. d
14. c
15. b
16. a

D. 1. He says he's got to see you right now.
He says he's got to speak to you right now.
He says he has to speak to you right now.
He claims he has to speak to you right now.
He claims he has to speak to you as soon as possible.

2. It's about a woman who showed up at the plant this morning.
   It's about a woman who showed up at the plant last year.
   It's about a woman who worked at the plant last year.
   It's about a doctor who worked at the plant last year.
   It's about a doctor who worked in the hospital last year.

3. That must be the head of the company.
   That may be the head of the company.
   That may be the director of the company.
   He may be the director of the company.
   He may be the director of the project.

4. He's been bothering me for two hours.
   He's been bothering me all day long.
   They've been bothering me all day long.
   They've been bothering me since this morning.
   They've been annoying us since this morning.

5. Don't you know the correct procedures?
   Doesn't he know the correct procedures?
   Doesn't he know the correct method?
   Didn't she know the correct method?
   Didn't she learn the correct method?

E. **There is no rule for when to use** do **or** make. **Unfortunately, these expressions have to be learned as you go along.**

   1. makes
   2. does
   3. make
   4. does
   5. does
   6. makes
   7. makes
   8. make

F. 1. to
   2. for
   3. at
   4. to
   5. of
   6. on
   7. with
   8. about

9 AN ADVERTISING CAMPAIGN

A. Suggested Answers

1. He wants to have a saturation campaign through the media.
2. Bill isn't in favor of the general strategy because it will cost too much.
3. Bill is against jingles because Allgood does not sell to the public.
4. He feels Bill does not appreciate his ideas.

B. 1. c   5. a
     2. a   6. c
     3. c   7. b
     4. c   8. b

C. 1. d   5. d   9. c   13. c
     2. c   6. c   10. a   14. d
     3. a   7. b   11. d   15. b
     4. b   8. a   12. b   16. a

D. 1. You've got the new advertising campaign all figured out.
You've got next year's advertising campaign all figured out.
She's got next year's advertising campaign all figured out.
She's got next year's budget all figured out.
She's got next year's budget completely figured out.

     2. It's going to ruin the company's image.
It will ruin the company's image.
It will hurt the company's image.
It will hurt the manager's image.
It will hurt the manager's plan.

     3. There's a limit on how much we can pay.
There's a limit on how many people we can pay.
There's a limit on how many people we can hire.
They've put a limit on how many people we can hire.
They've put a ceiling on how many people we can hire.

     4. We've thought of a jingle that will make Allgood a household word.
We've thought of a jingle that will make Allgood famous.
We've thought of an idea that will make Allgood famous.
We've thought of an idea that will make Allgood a fortune.
We've thought of an idea that could cost us a fortune.

     5. Are you sure you'd like me to go on?
Are you sure you'd like me to continue?
Are you positive you'd like me to continue?
Are you positive you'd like him to continue?
Are you positive you'd like him to finish?

E. 1. The advertising manager is responsible for promoting a company's products. He or she uses advertising media such as radio, TV, newspapers, trade fairs, etc.

     2. The general manager is responsible for the efficient and proper organization and operation of a company.

198

3. The personnel manager is responsible for hiring and firing employees, helping their promotion within the company, and looking after their welfare.

4. The comptroller is responsible for the financial affairs of the company.

F. 1. to, about, by
   2. to, for, by or by, for, to
   3. at, on, at, on
   4. of, for, in

G. 1. e, g, h, i   4. a, b, d
   2. c, d   5. b, c, d, f
   3. a, c, d   6. b, f, h

10 A BOARD MEETING

A. Suggested Answers

1. The business of the day is to discuss the new line of wrenches and screwdrivers.
2. The company needs to advertise.
3. He thinks that they need completely new names for their products.
4. She doesn't like Mr. Sutherland's suggestions; she thinks the quality and craftsmanship of the products should be emphasized.
5. Bill brings the meeting back to order by suggesting that incidentals be put aside until decisions are made on the campaign.

B. 1. b   5. c
   2. a   6. a
   3. a   7. c
   4. b   8. b

C. 1. b   5. d   9. b   13. c   17. b
   2. c   6. c   10. d   14. a   18. d
   3. d   7. b   11. a   15. d   19. c
   4. a   8. a   12. c   16. b   20. a

D. 1. Shall we adjourn, ladies and gentlemen?
      Shall we vote, ladies and gentlemen?
      Shall we open the discussion, ladies and gentlemen?
      Shall I open the discussion, ladies and gentlemen?
      Shall I get started, ladies and gentlemen?

2. Our study shows there's a great potential market for our products.
   Our study indicates there's a great potential market for our products.
   Our study indicates there's a great potential market for our new line.
   Our study indicates there's an excellent market for our new line.
   Our study indicates there exists an excellent market for our new line.

3. He's worked out an exciting campaign for us.
   He's proposed an exciting campaign for us.
   He's proposed an exciting scheme for us.
   He's come up with an exciting scheme for us.
   He's come up with a profitable scheme for us.

4. We should emphasize the excellence of our products.
   We should stress the excellence of our products.
   We should stress the excellence of the design.
   They should stress the excellence of the design.
   They should stress the utility of the design.

5. I've come up with some really great ideas.
   I've come up with some really excellent ideas.
   I've come up with a few really excellent ideas.
   I've thought of a few really excellent ideas.
   We've thought of a few really excellent ideas.

E. 1. probability
    2. probability
    3. obligation
    4. probability
    5. obligation
    6. probability
    7. obligation
    8. probability

F. 1. must
    2. must
    3. mustn't
    4. must
    5. mustn't
    6. mustn't

11 AFTER THE BOARD MEETING

A. Suggested Answers

1. Yes, he was.
2. He might have presented the products on TV himself.
3. She probably won't be happy about them, but she knows what to expect.
4. The display stands and the promotional packets for the trade fair will keep Rod Milton busy.

B. 1. a   4. c
2. c   5. a
3. c   6. b

C. 1. d   5. c   9. c   13. d   17. c
2. a   6. d   10. d   14. c   18. d
3. b   7. a   11. a   15. b   19. a
4. c   8. b   12. b   16. a   20. b

D. 1. It could have been better.
It might have been better.
It might have been more difficult.
It should have been more difficult.
It should have been less expensive.

2. She won't be happy about the extra work.
She couldn't be happy about the extra work.
She couldn't be happy about the unexpected work.
She couldn't be happy about the unexpected delays.
She couldn't be happy about the unexpected budget cuts.

3. She knows what to say.
She's decided what to say.
They've decided what to say.
They've decided what to do.
They've discussed what to do.

4. I told her I was against the TV spot.
I told her I was against the radio spot.
I told her I was for the radio spot.
I told her I was for the commercial spot.
I told her I voted for the commercial spot.

5. You'll have more than enough to keep you going.
You'll have plenty to keep you going.
There's plenty to keep you going.
There's plenty to keep you occupied.
There's hardly anything to keep you occupied.

E. The expressions *must have, may have,* or *couldn't have* **are used to draw conclusions about the past when the exact facts are not known.** *Must have* **is used when the speaker thinks that something very probably is true.** *May have* **(or** *might have***) is used when the speaker thinks that something possibly is**

201

true. *Couldn't have* **is used when the speaker thinks that it is impossible for** **something to be true.**

1. couldn't have
2. must have
3. must have
4. may have
5. couldn't have
6. may have, may have

F. *Had to* expresses obligation in the past.

1. b
2. a
3. b
4. a
5. b
6. a

12 PATENTS

A. Suggested Answers

1. He was holding the "trump card" because he knew that Allgood was the first to patent the design.
2. It was patented years before.
3. They had only made slight improvements on an old design.

B.
1. a
2. a
3. c
4. c
5. b
6. a

C.
1. d
2. c
3. a
4. b
5. c
6. a
7. d
8. b
9. c
10. d
11. a
12. b
13. d
14. a
15. b
16. c
17. c
18. a
19. d
20. b

D. 1. I'm sorry, but I don't think that's quite accurate.
I'm sorry, but I don't think that's completely accurate.
I'm sorry, but I'm not convinced that's completely accurate.
I'm sorry, but I'm not convinced his reasoning is completely accurate.
I'm sorry, but I'm positive his reasoning is completely accurate.

2. My lawyer has discovered some interesting material.
My secretary has discovered some interesting material.
My secretary has discovered some interesting documents.
My secretary has found some interesting documents.
My secretary has found some important documents.

3. It's a design which was developed years ago.
   It's a design which was developed some time ago.
   It's a design which was approved some time ago.
   It's an invention which was approved some time ago.
   It's an invention which was approved last year.

4. We'll continue with our plans for the trade fair.
   We'll go on with our plans for the trade fair.
   We'll go on with our plans for the future.
   They'll go on with their plans for the future.
   They'll go on with their projects for the future. *or*
   They'll go on with their plans for the projects.

5. My company's experts will have to study these designs.
   My company's engineers will have to study these designs.
   My company's engineers will have to change these designs.
   My company's engineers will have to change these plans.
   My company's engineers must change these plans.

E. 1. up, down
   2. down, up
   3. up, down
   4. up, down, up
   5. up, up
   6. up, down

F. 1. away, back
   2. back
   3. away
   4. away, back
   5. back
   6. back
   7. away

13 SALES: PROBLEMS AND PERSPECTIVES

A. Suggested Answers

1. At first Andy suggests the fact that Allgood raised their prices two months earlier as the reason for reduced sales.
2. He's not convinced that Allgood will increase its market by selling lower quality products, but he feels it is something to think about.
3. He was sent to the boss's office to listen to his complaints.
4. He would like to see improvements in the shipping department.

B. 1. b
   2. c
   3. a
   4. a
   5. b
   6. b

C.

1. c	5. c	9. c	13. c	17. d
2. d	6. d	10. a	14. a	18. c
3. a	7. b	11. b	15. d	19. a
4. b	8. a	12. d	16. b	20. b

D. 1. How long have you been selling in your present territory?
How long have you been selling in this territory?
Since when have you been selling in this territory?
Since when has she been selling in this territory?
Since when has she been selling in this area?

2. I see your sales are up this quarter.
I noticed your sales are up this quarter.
I noticed your sales were up this quarter.
I noticed your sales were up last quarter.
I noticed your sales were up last week.

3. Our market is much too limited.
Our product is much too limited.
Our product is much too expensive.
Our screwdrivers are much too expensive.
Our screwdrivers are much too cheap.

4. We're making equipment for skilled professionals.
We're manufacturing equipment for skilled professionals.
We're manufacturing tools for skilled professionals.
We're selling tools for skilled professionals.
We're selling instruments for skilled professionals.

5. I dropped in at Johnson's Hardware to check on a bill.
I dropped in at Johnson's Hardware to see about a bill.
I dropped in at a hardware store to see about a bill.
I stopped in at a hardware store to see about a bill.
Andy stopped in at a hardware store to see about a bill.

E. 1. much   4. many
2. much   5. many
3. many*

    * *Media* is a plural noun, although colloquially it is often treated
    as a singular one.

F. *Too much* **is followed by a noun.** *Too* **is followed by an adjective.**

1. too   4. too much
2. too much   5. too
3. too

204

G. 1. hadn't he
2. haven't I
3. wouldn't it
4. could you

5. should he
6. did they
7. has it

14 INDUSTRIAL ACCIDENT

A. Suggested Answers

1. He was not wearing goggles.
2. The workers don't like the goggles because they're uncomfortable and they have trouble seeing the machinery through them.
3. He was on the delivery ramp.
4. He wants to get the facts straight.
5. The company is going to order better goggles.

B. 1. c   4. b
2. a   5. a
3. c   6. b

C. 1. c   5. d   9. c   13. c   17. d
2. a   6. a   10. d   14. d   18. b
3. d   7. b   11. b   15. a   19. a
4. b   8. c   12. a   16. b   20. c

D. 1. He's been working here for over a month.
He's been working in this town for over a month.
He's been living in this town for over a month.
They've been living in this town for over a month.
They've been living in New York for over a month.

2. He should know his responsibilities by now.
He should be aware of his responsibilities by now.
He should be aware of his obligations by now.
He should have fulfilled his obligations by now.
He should have fulfilled his obligations before.

3. They're having trouble using the machinery.
They're having trouble using the equipment.
They're having difficulty using the equipment.
The workers are having difficulty using the equipment.
The workers are having problems using the equipment.

4. Where were they at the time of the accident?
   Where were they during the accident?
   Where were they during the proceedings?
   Where was he during the proceedings?
   Where was he after the proceedings?

5. I just wanted to get the facts straight.
   I only wanted to get the facts straight.
   I only wanted to get the details straight.
   I only tried to get the details straight.
   They only tried to get the details straight.

E. 1. He doesn't want to succeed very much.
2. They don't emphasize safety regulations very much.
3. We don't like TV commercials very much.
4. She doesn't enjoy trade fairs very much.
5. Does it matter very much if they don't wear the goggles?

F. 1. The company's image has changed a lot over the last few years.
2. He'll get a lot out of it.
3. I liked the ads we saw a lot.
4. It'll cost a lot.
5. He sells a lot on Fridays.
6. There's a lot to be said for the new system.

15 STOLEN MONEY

A. Suggested Answers

1. Pat has come to see Anna because there is $2000 missing from the company's account.
2. She thinks the cashier has accepted a check without proper verification.
3. She noticed a rather unusual deposit—several large checks and almost no cash—on a day when the company had received a lot of cash.

B. 1. c   4. b
2. b   5. a
3. c   6. c

C. 1. b   5. d   9. c   13. c   17. d
2. c   6. c   10. a   14. d   18. c
3. a   7. a   11. b   15. b   19. a
4. d   8. b   12. d   16. a   20. b

D. 1. Since when do we have a policy of rejecting checks?
Since when do you have a policy of rejecting checks?
Since when do you have a policy of rejecting customers?
Since when do you have a policy of being rude to customers?
Since when does he have a policy of being rude to customers?

2. You'd better tell me the whole truth.
You'd better tell them the whole truth.
You'd better tell them the details.
She'd better tell them the details.
She had to tell them the details.

3. That doesn't prove it was an inside job.
That doesn't prove it was a bad job.
That doesn't prove it was a bad deal.
That doesn't prove it was a fraudulent deal.
That doesn't prove it was a fraudulent scheme.

4. I think that somebody here took the cash.
I think that somebody here took the money.
I suspect that somebody here took the money.
I suspect that somebody here took the check.
I suspect that somebody here substituted the check.

5. We had better notify Bill immediately.
We had better notify Bill at once.
We had better notify him at once.
We must notify him at once.
We must tell him at once.

E. 1. over, across   4. over, across
2. through, over   5. through, over
3. over, across   6. through, across

F. **The simple present tense indicates a habitual or repeated action. The** *going to* **future tense indicates an action that is about to happen. Remember that** *can,* *must,* **and** *may* **have no** *going to* **form.**

1. When I leave on Fridays I leave my worries behind me.
2. I always plan something special for Friday evenings.
3. Take this Friday for example: I'm going to meet a few of my friends after work.
4. We're going to have a few drinks, Chinese food, and then we're going to go to the movies.
5. There's going to be (*or* There's) a sneak preview of a new film this Friday, but I can't remember the name.

207

16 MUNICIPAL LAW

A. Suggested Answers

1. Allgood has erected an advertising sign that was in violation of the city bylaws.
2. Bill has stopped by Judy's office to see what's happening about the sign.
3. Peter thinks the case raises an important point of law.
4. He wants to know what Allgood is going to do with the sign.
5. She thinks the decision is going to be in Allgood's favor.

B. 1. c   4. c
     2. b   5. a
     3. c   6. b

C. 1. c   5. d   9. d   13. c
     2. d   6. c   10. c   14. d
     3. a   7. a   11. a   15. b
     4. b   8. b   12. b   16. a

D. 1. We can't understand what all the fuss is about.
     We can't see what all the fuss is about.
     We can't see what all the fighting is about.
     We can't see what all the fighting is for.
     We can't see what all the arguing is for.

2. It's necessary to clear up inconsistencies.
     It's necessary to avoid inconsistencies.
     It's necessary to avoid mistakes.
     It's necessary to correct mistakes.
     It's difficult to correct mistakes.

3. I don't want to deal with this legal terminology.
     I don't want to deal with this legal business.
     I don't want to deal with this legal setup.
     I don't want to be involved with this legal setup.
     I would hate to be involved with this legal setup.

4. I definitely expect the decision to be in our favor.
     I definitely want the decision to be in our favor.
     I definitely want the verdict to be in our favor.
     I definitely don't want the verdict to be in our favor.
     I definitely don't want the verdict to be in their favor.

5. Tell me when the court has decided.
Tell me when the court is meeting.
Tell me when the board of directors is meeting.
Let me know when the board of directors is meeting.
Let us know when the board of directors is meeting.

E. The meanings of the present perfect tense and the present perfect progressive tense are often so similar that they can be used interchangeably (i.e., *I've played golf with you every day this week. I've been playing golf with you every day this week.*). **Both tenses refer to actions begun in the past and continuing up through or up to the present.**

There are, however, subtle differences in use and meaning. The present perfect progressive generally conveys the feeling of an uninterrupted action or an action that has been done repeatedly in the recent past, while the present perfect usually conveys the feeling that the action has just finished or has just been interrupted.

Jim has been playing well this morning. **He is still playing well.**
Jim has played well this morning. **He has stopped playing now.**

Only the present perfect tense can be used when a specific number of things or times is included (i.e., *Jim has won three games today.*).

Bill: b, a
Jim: b
Bill: a, b
     a, a
Jim: a, b

F. 1. He always had to buy them ice-cream cones.
2. She is seldom on time.
3. They never have the right to choose.
4. Does he often behave like that?
5. She sometimes does it on purpose.
6. Does he ever ask you about it?
7. They occasionally have a day in the country.
8. She is usually well informed.

17 A COMPLAINT

A. Suggested Answers

1. He says that the order was not complete.

2. He checked it himself.
3. Allgood could solve the problem easily by looking at Helke's inventory records.
4. He's going to deliver the next order himself and have a look around while he's there.

B. 1. a   4. c
    2. a   5. a
    3. a   6. b

C. 1. c   5. d   9. d   13. d   17. c
    2. d   6. c   10. c   14. c   18. d
    3. b   7. a   11. a   15. a   19. a
    4. a   8. b   12. b   16. b   20. b

D. 1. The shipment was undamaged when it left here.
The shipment was undamaged when it arrived here.
The shipment was in perfect condition when it arrived here.
The merchandise was in perfect condition when it arrived here.
The merchandise was in perfect condition when it was delivered.

2. Someone in their warehouse has to make out a receipt.
Someone in their warehouse has to make out a statement.
Someone in their accounting department has to make out a statement.
Someone in their accounting department is supposed to make out a statement.
Someone in their accounting department is supposed to make out a bill.

3. I guess it's put in a warehouse and used as needed.
I guess it's put in a stockroom and used as needed.
I guess it's put in a stockroom and used as required.
I guess it's kept in a stockroom and used as required.
I imagine it's kept in a stockroom and used as required.

4. There must be a listing of this order at the warehouse.
There must be a listing of this order in the directory.
There must be a listing of this company in the directory.
There must be a description of this company in the directory.
There has got to be a description of this company in the directory.

5. Let me know if you come up with anything.
Let me know as soon as you come up with anything.
Let me know as soon as you find out anything.
Call me as soon as you find out anything.
Call me as soon as you find out what happened.

E.

1. advertisement	6. pages
2. representative	7. public relations
3. memorandum	8. street
4. brothers	9. road
5. cash or collect on delivery	10. incorporated

F. 1. Protective clothing must be worn in the workshop.
2. Only authorized persons are permitted in this area.
3. Smoking is not permitted in the work area.
4. All accidents must be reported to the personnel manager.

18 CUSTOMER RELATIONS

A. Suggested Answers

1. They could not prove that Mr. Helke was wrong.
2. Helke said Allgood was inefficient, incompetent, and negligent.
3. Emil lost his temper when Helke called Allgood a bunch of crooks.
4. No, he's not.

B.

1. b		4. a	
2. c		5. c	
3. b		6. c	

C.

1. c	5. b	9. b	13. c	17. c
2. a	6. d	10. d	14. a	18. d
3. d	7. a	11. a	15. d	19. b
4. b	8. c	12. c	16. b	20. a

D. 1. Let me know what's going on as soon as possible.
Let me know what's going on as soon as you can.
Let me know what's going on when you can.
Tell them what's going on when you can.
Tell them what's going on when they call.

2. As soon as I walked in Helke started blaming Allgood.
After I walked in Helke started blaming Allgood.
After I walked in Helke started blaming the staff.
(After I walked in the staff started blaming Allgood.)
After I walked in Helke started talking about the staff.

(After I walked in the staff started talking about Allgood.)
After I got there Helke started talking about the staff.
(After I got there the staff started talking about Allgood.)

3. We got a phone call from him about a half an hour ago.
   We got a phone call from them about a half an hour ago.
   We got a phone call from them only a half an hour ago.
   We got a phone call from them only yesterday.
   We got a telegram from them only yesterday.

4. You're probably the first employee who's told him off.
   You're probably the first employee who's argued with him.
   You're definitely the first employee who's argued with him.
   You're definitely the first customer who's argued with him.
   You're definitely the first customer who's agreed with him.

5. Helke found out that there were several things missing.
   Helke found out that there were several things damaged.
   Helke discovered that there were several things damaged.
   Helke discovered that there were several items damaged.
   Helke discovered that there were several items lost in transit.

E. 1. still
        2. already
        3. yet
        4. already
        5. still
        6. already
        7. still
        8. yet

F. 1. income
        2. outcome
        3. input
        4. outlet
        5. upkeep
        6. breakdown
        7. turnover

19 ON THE JOB

A. Suggested Answers

1. He studies his territory and his prospective customers.
2. The display stand allows customers to see at a glance the wide range of tools available and their different uses.
3. Yes, he thinks it will take up too much space.
4. He has worked out a floor plan of the hardware department.
5. He says that Mr. McAdam knows what's going on in the world of business.

B.
1. c 4. c
2. c 5. a
3. b 6. a

C.
1. c   5. c   9. d   13. d   17. b
2. d   6. a   10. b   14. c   18. d
3. a   7. d   11. a   15. a   19. a
4. b   8. b   12. c   16. b   20. c

D. 1. The customer can see at a glance the wide variety of tools available.
The client can see at a glance the wide variety of tools available.
The client can see at a glance the wide variety of tools on hand.
The client can see at once the wide variety of tools on hand.
The client can see at once the wide variety of goods on hand.

2. I have to admit there's more available than I thought.
I have to agree there's more available than I thought.
I have to agree there's more on display than I thought.
I have to agree there's more on display than I supposed.
I have to agree there's more at our disposal than I supposed.
(I have to agree there's more on display than at our disposal.)

3. This stand will take up an awful lot of room.
This project will take up an awful lot of room.
This project will take up too much room.
This project will take up too much time.
This project will use up too much time.

4. We've already worked out an outline for you.
We've just worked out an outline for you.
We've just prepared an outline for you.
We've just prepared a schedule for you.
We've just prepared a schedule for our visitors.

5. It's certainly a pleasure dealing with someone who knows what's going on.
It's certainly an honor dealing with someone who knows what's going on.
It's certainly an honor working with someone who knows what's going on.
It's certainly an honor working with someone who understands what's going on.
It's certainly an honor working with people who understand what's going on.
(It's certainly an honor working with someone who understands people.)

E.
1. I'll order
2. had thought
3. hear
4. got
5. started
6. I'll go
7. discover
8. I'll let

F. 1a:2a *or* 2b   1d:2f
    1b:2d   1e:2e
    1c:2a *or* 2b *or* 2f   1f:2c

20   AN EXPORT INITIATIVE

A. Suggested Answers

1. The last time Allgood tried to export, they wasted a lot of time and money.
2. The market for hardware in Bustani is developing rapidly and their credit status is excellent.
3. The Department of Commerce is helping Allgood get the necessary licenses and permits and has promised to process Allgood's documents without delay.
4. Yes, because the market looks promising.

B.

1. a	4. a
2. c	5. b
3. b	6. b

C.

1. c	5. d	9. b	13. c	17. a
2. a	6. a	10. c	14. d	18. c
3. d	7. b	11. d	15. b	19. d
4. b	8. c	12. a	16. a	20. b

D.
  1. I'm not in favor of this project of yours.
     I'm not in favor of this project of hers.
     I wasn't in favor of this project of hers.
     I wasn't in favor of that project of hers.
     I wasn't against that project of hers.

  2. We're trying to maintain our markets right here.
     We're trying to maintain a base right here.
     We're trying to establish a base right here.
     We're trying to establish a base in this area.
     We would like to establish a base in this area.

  3. They sent a telegram to the commercial attaché in Bustani.
     They sent a telegram to the head office in Bustani.
     They sent a telegram to the head office in New York.
     They sent the documents to the head office in New York.
     They forwarded the documents to the head office in New York.

4. They promised to process our documents immediately.
They intend to process our documents immediately.
They intend to process our contracts immediately.
They intend to settle our contracts immediately.
They intend to settle our contracts promptly.

5. The special report from the attaché should be sent off by Friday.
The financial report from the attaché should be sent off by Friday.
The financial report from the attaché should be sent off by next week.
The financial report from the branch office should be sent off by next week.
The financial report from the branch office must be sent off by next week.

E. 1. b   3. b, c
     2. a, b, c, d   4. b, c

F. 1. buy   5. bought, asked or found, carry
     2. become   6. becoming, became
     3. have   7. became, are going to be
     4. buy or give

21 EXPORT PROSPECTS

A. Suggested Answers

1. Fred is looking good and has a sun tan.
2. At least one of Allgood's bids is in the lead because of Allgood's competitive pricing, flexibility of contract terms, and product availability.
3. He found an agent who is experienced in representing foreign accounts.
4. He feels very pleased.
5. "Carte blanche" means to have a free hand to do as one wants. Fred would find this useful now because he has an appointment with the Bustani Foreign Trade Mission, and he won't want to have to turn to Bill for permission to proceed.

B. 1. c   4. a
     2. b   5. c
     3. b   6. b

C. 1. d   5. d   9. d   13. c
     2. c   6. c   10. c   14. a
     3. a   7. a   11. b   15. d
     4. b   8. b   12. a   16. b

D. 1. Because of our low prices, our bid is in the lead.
Due to our low prices, our bid is in the lead.
Due to our low estimate, our bid is in the lead.
Due to our low estimate, our bid has a good chance.
Due to our low estimate, our project has a good chance.

2. She's very experienced in dealing with foreign accounts.
She's very experienced in dealing with foreign contracts.
She's very experienced in dealing with overseas contracts.
She's very experienced in dealing with overseas investments.
She's very adept at dealing with overseas investments.

3. The main thing is to secure those government contracts.
The main thing is to get those government contracts.
The main thing is to get those municipal contracts.
The main thing is to get those municipal bonds.
The main thing is to buy those municipal bonds.

4. They'll be the most important orders we've ever received.
They'll be the most important contracts we've ever received.
They'll be the most important contracts we've ever signed.
They'll be the most important contracts we've ever negotiated.
They'll be the most difficult contracts we've ever negotiated.

5. Let me know if there's anything you want.
Tell me if there's anything you want.
Tell me if there's anything you require.
Tell me if there's anything we can do.
Tell me if there's something we can do.

E. 1. met   4. found
2. arrived   5. visit
3. was

F. 1. up, down   4. up
2. down   5. out
3. out   6. over

22 A JUBILANT REACTION

A. Suggested Answers

1. He hoped Allgood would be lucky and get the contract.
2. Allgood got the contract for the municipal development program.

3. Fred was right about exporting.
4. They are going to have dinner at The Four Seasons with their wives.
5. Fred wants Allgood to build a factory in Bustani.

B. 1. a   4. c
    2. a   5. c
    3. b   6. a

C. 1. c   5. c   9. d   13. d
    2. d   6. a   10. c   14. a
    3. a   7. d   11. b   15. b
    4. b   8. b   12. a   16. c

D. 1. I'd like you to come to my office right away.
      I'd like you to come to my apartment right away.
      I'd like you to come to my apartment immediately.
      I'd like you to come to my department immediately.
      We'd like you to come to our department immediately.

    2. A letter's just arrived from the Austrian government.
      This letter's just arrived from the Austrian government.
      This telegram's just arrived from the Austrian government.
      Another telegram's just arrived from the Austrian government.
      Another telegram's just come from the Austrian government.

    3. It's the contract we negotiated for the municipal development program.
      It's the deal we negotiated for the municipal development program.
      It's the deal we negotiated for Black and Sons.
      It's the deal we worked out for Black and Sons.
      It's the report we worked out for Black and Sons.

    4. It was really all your fault.
      It is really all your fault.
      This is really all your fault.
      This is really all his fault.
      This is probably all his fault.

    5. It would be a perfect time to tell me why we should build.
      It would be a perfect time to tell him why we should build.
      It would be a perfect time to tell him why we should expand.
      Tomorrow would be a perfect time to tell him why we should expand.
      Tomorrow would be a perfect time to explain to him why we should expand.

E. **When the present tense of the verb is used in the** *if* **clause, the future tense is used in the main clause; when a past tense of the verb is used in the** *if* **clause,** *would, could,* **or** *might* **is used in the main clause.**

1. He'd be much happier if he didn't have to travel so much.
2. If we don't take a gamble we'll never expand our sales.
3. We'll secure the contracts if we reduce our prices.
4. If we could produce tools as cheaply as our competitors we would have bigger sales.
5. If she were given a promotion she would earn a higher salary.
6. We'll celebrate at The Four Seasons if we get the contract.
7. They'll send the shipment out tomorrow if the money and documents arrive.

F.
1. Do you know what's going on?
2. Do you know where Fred is?
3. Do you know why Fred isn't here?
4. Do you know what it is?
5. Do you know who Mr. Samson is?
6. Do you know when Judy's coming back?
7. Do you know how they did it?
8. Do you know who was right?
9. Do you know whose story I would believe?
10. Do you know which companies are building in Bustani?

23 MARGARET'S ILLNESS

A. Suggested Answers

1. She has the flu and can't go to the office.
2. Helen Glavac is going to help Bill while Margaret is sick.
3. No.

B.
1. b	4. b
2. b	5. b
3. c	6. b

C.
1. d	5. c	9. d	13. c
2. c	6. d	10. c	14. d
3. a	7. b	11. b	15. a
4. b	8. a	12. a	16. b

D. 1. He said I can't go out for a few days.
He said I can't go away for a few days.
He said I should go away for a few days.
He said I should go away for a week.
I was told I should go away for a week.

2. I've asked the accountant to help you.
I've ordered the accountant to help you.
He ordered the accountant to help you.
He told the accountant to help you.
He told the accountant to work with you.

3. Take a look at the file and see if you have enough information.
Check the file and see if you have enough information.
Check the file and see if you have sufficient information.
Examine the file and see if you have sufficient information.
Examine the documents and see if you have sufficient information.

4. Perhaps you'll have to postpone it.
Perhaps you'll have to finish it.
Maybe you'll have to finish it.
I'm sure you'll have to finish it.
I'm sure you'll have to forget about it.

5. What we have to do could wait until next week.
What we have to do could wait until tomorrow.
What we have to do could be postponed until tomorrow.
What we have to do could be postponed until next year.
Everything we have to do could be postponed until next year.

E. 1. If industry doesn't look for overseas markets, it won't be able to expand.
2. If you don't know how your competitors operate, you can't sell.
3. If the consultation were free and tax deductible, we would go.
4. If you want that promotion you will have to work harder.
5. If we had a contingency plan we could solve the problem easily.

F. 1. mustn't
2. don't have to
3. mustn't
4. don't have to
5. don't have to

24 WHAT FINALLY HAPPENED

A. Suggested Answers

1. Agricultural equipment is being supplied by a European country in exchange for cotton and coffee exports.
2. Yes, they have.
3. Allgood has become a household word because they award the Allgood Trophy to the most promising young golfer in the United States.

B.

1. c	4. b
2. c	5. c
3. a	6. c

C.

1. c	5. c	9. c	13. c
2. d	6. a	10. d	14. d
3. a	7. d	11. a	15. b
4. b	8. b	12. b	16. a

D.
1. It was supplied by an African country in exchange for cotton.
   It was supplied by an African country in exchange for oil.
   It was furnished by an African country in exchange for oil.
   It was furnished by an African company in exchange for oil.
   It was furnished by an Asian company in exchange for oil.

2. The company has a number of factories throughout the world.
   The company has many factories throughout the world.
   The company has many factories all around the world.
   The company has many factories everywhere in the world.
   The company has many manufacturing plants everywhere in the world.

3. Its products are made by special arrangement in Germany.
   Its tools are made by special arrangement in Germany.
   Its tools are made by special arrangement in Bustani.
   Its tools are made by special arrangement in foreign countries.
   Its tools are manufactured by special arrangement in foreign countries.

4. The company has become well-known by awarding a golf trophy.
   The company has become very popular by awarding a golf trophy.
   The company has become very popular by awarding a scholarship.
   The company has become very popular by giving a scholarship.
   The company became very popular by giving a scholarship.

E. 1. The goods were sent by air freight.
2. A new distributing agent was found.
3. The new design was registered in several Asian countries.
4. The detailed description can (is to) be found in paragraph 4, subsection 3b.
5. The complete order was dispatched on February 4.

F. 1. putting, go
2. kept
3. putting
4. go, come
5. put, come
6. was
7. got
8. put

H. Dear Sir or Madam:
One of your representatives has informed me that your company is going to market a new range of wrenches in the near future. I should be very grateful if you would send me some information concerning this product. The representative also informed me that your company is going to sell a new screwdriver. Would you tell me more about this new product?

Thanking you in advance, I am,
Sincerely yours,
B. Carlton

25 BILL'S RETIREMENT

A. Suggested Answers

1. Fred will be in charge of Allgood from now on because Bill is retiring.
2. Bill wants to improve his golf handicap, travel in the East, and visit his son in Los Angeles.
3. They are having a farewell banquet for him.
4. Yes, Fred knows the company. He has had a lot of experience and has a dynamic approach to business.

B. 1. a
2. c
3. b
4. a
5. b
6. c

C. 1. c
2. a
3. d
4. b
5. c
6. d
7. b
8. a
9. d
10. c
11. a
12. b
13. c
14. d
15. a
16. b

D. 1. Our representatives are hoping to leave in about a month.
Our representatives are hoping to leave in a few weeks.
Our representatives are hoping to return in a few weeks.
Our representatives are hoping to return after a few weeks.
Our representatives expect to return after a few weeks.

2. I've always been fascinated by oriental rugs.
I've always been interested in oriental rugs.
I've always been interested in traveling.
I've never been interested in traveling.
We've never been interested in traveling.

3. I plan to spend some time in Bali.
I plan to spend a few weeks in Bali.
I plan to spend a few weeks in the West.
I plan to stay a few weeks in the West.
We'd like to stay a few weeks in the West.

4. I'll call you the next time there's a recession.
I'll call you the next time there's an overdue shipment.
I'll call you every time there's an overdue shipment.
I'll call you every time we have an overdue shipment.
I'll call you every time we have a strike.

5. I must admit I'm pleased you're taking over.
I must admit I'm pleased you're replacing me.
I must admit I'm delighted you're replacing me.
I have to admit I'm delighted you're replacing me.
I have to admit I'm relieved you're replacing me.

E. 1. on
2. about
3. in
4. to
5. at
6. to, on
7. about

F. 1. The position of the modifying phrase, *with references*, is incorrect. The phrase modifies *man*, not *truck*, and should be placed after the word it modifies. *Wanted: man with references to drive truck.*

2. The position of the modifying phrase, *on a motor scooter*, is incorrect. The phrase modifies *businessman*, not *bus*, and should be placed after the word it modifies. *The businessman on a motor scooter was hit by a bus.*

3. The position of the modifying phrase, *on safari*, is incorrect. The phrase modifies *two hunters*, not *tigers*, and should be placed after the word it modifies. *Two hunters on safari were attacked by tigers.*

4. The position of the modifying phrase, *in the blue suit,* is incorrect. The phrase modifies *woman,* not *table,* and should be placed after the word it modifies. *The woman in the blue suit ordered the table with mahogony legs.*

5. The position of the modifying phrase, *with a beard,* is incorrect. The phrase modifies *the customer,* not *french fries,* and should be placed after the word it modifies. *The customer with a beard ordered a hamburger and french fries.*

GLOSSARY

The following is a list of the business-related vocabulary used in the text. Definitions are limited to the way in which the words and expressions are used in the book.

Abbreviations: *n.* noun, *v.* verb, *adj.* adjective, *adv.* adverb

account (*n*)   any business relationship involving the exchange of money or credit
accountant (*n*)   a person who keeps books or examines accounts
adjourn (*v*)   to suspend proceedings (e.g., of a meeting) to another time or place
administrative assistant (*n*)   supervisor of office routine work; a person who assists an administrator in organizing and completing work
advertisement (ad) (*n*)   a public notice, as in a newspaper, or on a radio or television program to proclaim the qualities and advantages of a product so as to increase sales
advertising agency (*n*)   an agency to plan and design advertisements for the purpose of promoting sales or interest
advertising campaign (*n*)   an organized series of advertisement activities to attain some commercial goal
advertising manager (*n*)   person in charge of advertising activities in a company
advisory board (*n*)   an organized body of administrators having or exercising power to advise or offer counsel
agenda (*n*)   a list of things to be done or matters to be discussed
agent (*n*)   a person authorized to act on behalf of another person or group
air freight (*n*)   a system of transporting goods by aircraft; the amount charged for such transportation
appeal (*n*)   a request for reconsideration
applicant (*n*)   a person who applies for something (e.g., for a job)
application (*n*)   a formal written request, as for a job
appointment (*n*)   an agreement to meet at a certain time and place; the act of appointing or designating for an office or position
assistant (*n*)   helper; a person who gives aid and support
attaché (*n*)   a person officially attached to a diplomatic mission or staff in a special capacity (e.g., military or commercial attaché)
attorney (*n*)   lawyer
balance of payments (*n*)   the systematic recording of a nation's total payments to foreign countries and its total receipts from foreign countries
bid (*n*)   an offer to pay or accept a price, as at an auction or in competition for a contract

bill (statement) (n)   a statement listing charges for goods delivered or services rendered

billboard (n)   a structure, usually outdoors, for the display of notices or advertisements

board meeting (n)   the meeting of an organized official body

board of directors (n)   a group of directors (e.g., as of a corporation) who supervise or manage a company

board of trade (n)   a board or an organization that regulates, promotes, supervises, or protects commercial or business interests

bond (n)   a certificate of debt, usually issued by a government or corporation, guaranteeing payment of the original investment plus interest by a specified future date

boss (n)   a person who employs or supervises others; one's superior

branch office (n)   a local unit of an organization or corporation

brand (n)   a mark or label identifying a product or a manufacturer

brochure (n)   a small pamphlet or booklet

budget (n)   an estimate of the amount of money that can be spent within a given period of time

budget cuts (n)   budgetary restrictions or reductions

business premises (n)   the grounds of a house or building used for business

bylaws (n)   laws made by a city or an organization to govern internal affairs

cable (n)   cablegram; telegram sent by submarine cable

call (n)   telephone call

campaign (n)   an organized series of activities to attain a goal (e.g., advertising or political campaign)

capital (n)   the total amount of money, stocks, or property owned or used by an individual or corporation

carte blanche (n)   full authority; unrestricted power to act at one's own discretion

City Council (n)   the governing body of a city; municipal government

client (n)   customer

colleague (n)   a fellow member of a profession or staff

commerce (n)   the buying and selling of goods, especially on a large scale, as between cities or nations; business; trade

commercial (n)   a paid advertisement on radio or television

commercial attaché (n)   a person officially attached to a diplomatic mission or staff in charge of his or her country's commercial activities with a foreign country

commission (n)   a fee or percentage allowed to a salesperson or agent for his or her services

committee (n)   a group of people chosen to consider some matter or to function in a certain capacity

commodity (n)   any article of commerce

commodity prices (n)   in general, the price of articles bought and sold in commerce

company (n)   a business enterprise; a firm

competition (n)   a striving against another or others as for a prize, profit, or position; rivalry between two or more businesses striving for the same customer or market

competitor (n)   one who competes, as in games or in business

comptroller (*n*) an officer appointed to examine and verify accounts and to supervise the financial affairs of a corporation or of a governmental body

conference room (*n*) a meeting room

consultant (*n*) a person who gives expert or professional advice

consumer (*n*) a person who acquires goods, products, and services; a buyer

contingency plan (*n*) a plan or procedure that may be adopted in the event of a future change or emergency

contract (*n*) a formal agreement between two or more parties, especially one that is written and enforceable by law

craftsman (*n*) a skilled worker who practices a craft by occupation

craftsmanship (*n*) skilled workmanship

credit (*n*) an amount placed by a bank at a customer's disposal; confidence in a purchaser's ability and intention to pay or fulfill financial obligations at some future time

credit standing or status (*n*) reputation for meeting financial obligations

customer (*n*) one who buys goods or services, especially on a regular basis

data (*n*) facts or figures, especially those organized for analysis or used as the basis for a decision

deadline (*n*) a time limit, as for payment of a debt or completion of an assignment

deductible (*adj*) allowable as a tax deduction

deficit (*n*) the amount by which a sum of money falls short of the required or expected amount; a shortage

delivery (*n*) the act of delivering or taking something to a place or person

delivery ramp (*n*) inclined passageway of a building to load or unload trucks

delivery receipt (*n*) a written acknowledgment of the delivery of goods

department (*n*) a distinct part or division of a large organization (e.g., accounting department), having a specialized function and personnel

Department of Commerce (*n*) department of the United States federal government that promotes and develops domestic and foreign trade

deposit (*v*) to entrust money for safekeeping in a bank; to give partial payment or security

director (*n*) one who supervises, controls, or manages; a member of a board of persons who control or govern the affairs of an institution or corporation

display (*n*) an exhibition, as of merchandise, designed to advertise

display stand (*n*) a stall, booth, or counter where goods are displayed

distributing agent (*n*) a person or firm designated to sell or deliver an item or line of merchandise, especially to customers in a specific area

distribution (*n*) the marketing, transporting, and merchandising of goods

document (*n*) a written or printed paper giving information or evidence about a particular object or matter; a legal or official paper

efficiency (*n*) the quality of being efficient; effectiveness

electronics firm (*n*) an establishment dealing in devices, circuits, or systems developed through electronics

employee (*n*) one who works for another in return for salary or wages

employer (*n*) a person or a business firm that employs persons for wages or salary

enterprise (*n*) a project or undertaking, especially an important or difficult one; a business

estimate (*n*) a rough calculation of value

executive (*n*)   a person having administrative or managerial authority in a corporation or institution

exhibit (*v*)   to present for the public to view   (*n*)   a display

exhibition (*n*)   the act of exhibiting, especially publicly

experience (*n*)   the period of time that one has been directly occupied in something; the knowledge or skill so derived (e.g., experience in selling)

export (*v*)   to send or sell merchandise to other countries

factory (*n*)   a building or group of buildings in which goods are manufactured; a plant

fair (*n*)   a periodic and usually competitive gathering for the buying and selling of goods; a market

finances (*n*)   money resources, especially of a government or corporate body

financial policy (*n*)   a course or plan for the management of financial matters (e.g., the financial policy of a government, company, etc.)

fire (*v*)   to terminate the employment of another person; to dismiss from a position

firm (*n*)   a partnership of two or more persons for conducting business; a business establishment

floorplan (*n*)   a scale diagram of a room or building drawn as if seen from above

fraud (*n*)   willful deceit or cheating to secure unfair or unlawful gain

general manager (*n*)   the director of a business or other enterprise

gross national product (*n*)   the total market value of all goods and services produced in a country during a year

hardware (*n*)   metal goods and utensils such as locks, tools, and cutlery

hot item (*n*)   so new as not to have lost freshness, excitement; enjoying popularity; readily salable

import (*v*)   to bring in or buy merchandise from a foreign country for trade or sale

industrial accident (*n*)   an accident that takes place in a plant or a shop during work

industrial firm (*n*)   a business establishment dealing with manufacturing

intercom (*n*)   an intercommunication system, as between two rooms

interest (*n*)   a sum paid or charged for the use or borrowing of money

interview (*n*)   a conversation conducted by an employer or reporter with a person from whom information is expected; a face-to-face meeting for the formal discussion of a matter, such as employment

inventory (*n*)   a detailed list of articles in one's possession; especially a periodic survey of all goods and materials in stock

investment (*n*)   the act of putting money into business for the purpose of profit

issue (*n*)   a point of discussion, debate, or dispute

jargon (*n*)   the technical or specialized language used among members of a particular trade, profession, class, or fellowship (e.g., legal jargon)

jingle (*n*)   a catchy short song or poem, especially one used for advertising

job (*n*)   anything that is to be done; work; a position in which one is employed

journal (*n*)   a periodical presenting news of a particular field (e.g., medical journal)

junior executive (*n*)   an executive who is lower in rank than a senior executive (see *executive*)

labor costs (*n*)   cost of the working force in a corporation

labor relations (*n*) relations between management and labor in business or industry

layoff (*n*) the suspension or dismissal of employees

legal jargon (*n*) specialized language used by people working in the law field

license (*n*) official or legal permission to do something

line (*n*) merchandise of a similar or related nature

loan (*n*) a sum of money lent with interest

maintenance costs (*n*) cost of upkeep

management (*n*) the art of managing; administration; the person or persons who manage a business establishment, organization, or institution

management team (*n*) the persons who manage a business establishment, organization, or institution

manager (*n*) one who directs or controls a business or other enterprise

manufacturer (*n*) a person or enterprise that makes or processes goods, especially on a large scale and with machinery

manufacturing company (*n*) firm whose business is to make or process goods

market (*n*) a place where there is a demand for goods

marketing (*n*) the total of activities involved in moving goods from producer to consumer including buying, selling, storing, transporting, and supplying market information

marketing director (*n*) one in charge of marketing activities; marketing manager

marketing manager (*n*) see *marketing director*

market report (*n*) a report on consumer preferences for goods and services

mass production (*n*) the manufacture of goods in large quantities, using standardized designs and often assembly-line techniques

media (*n*) a means of mass communication, such as newspapers, magazines, radio, or television

meeting (*n*) an assembly or gathering of persons for a special purpose

memo (*n*) short for memorandum

memorandum (*n*) a brief note or informal letter usually sent between departments in an office

merchandise (*n*) the bulk of commodities of commerce; goods that may be bought or sold

minutes (*n*) an official record of the proceedings of a meeting

motion (*n*) a formal proposal in a meeting (e.g., to make a motion)

municipal law (*n*) law legislated by a City Council or pertaining to a town or a city

negotiate (*v*) to bargain with another party in order to come to terms or to reach an agreement

office procedures (*n*) a set of established methods or forms for conducting office work

order (*n*) a commission or instruction to buy, sell, or supply something

packaging (*n*) the act, process, industry, art, or style of packing

patent (*n*) government protection which grants an inventor the exclusive right to make use of or sell an invention for a stated period of time

patent attorney (*n*) a lawyer who handles all matters concerning patents

patent bureau (*n*) (also *patent office*) a government agency in which claims for patents are studied and patents are issued and recorded

personnel (*n*) the persons employed in an organization, business, or service

personnel department (*n*)   a department in a business establishment or organization concerned with the employees of the company

personnel manager (*n*)   a person in charge of personnel and/or the personnel department

plant (*n*)   workshop or factory

policy (*n*)   any course or plan of action adopted by a business organization or governmental administration

position (*n*)   job, employment

procedure (*n*)   a set of established methods or forms for conducting a business

product (*n*)   anything produced, manufactured

production manager (*n*)   person in charge of the process of production in a business or manufacturing firm

productivity (*n*)   the degree of effectiveness of management in using labor and equipment

project (*n*)   something proposed or planned; a major undertaking, especially one involving a large sum of money

promotion (*n*)   an advancement in rank or responsibility; advertising or other publicity

promotional packet (*n*)   a small package made up of materials designed to promote a product

proposal (*n*)   something put forward for consideration or acceptance

quarter (*n*)   three months or a fourth of a year

raise (*n*)   an increase in salary

receipt (*n*)   a written acknowledgment that a specified article, sum of money, or delivery of goods has been received

receptionist (*n*)   a person employed chiefly to receive callers at the entrance of an office and answer the telephone

recession (*n*)   a moderate and temporary decline in economic activity

record (*n*)   a written account that serves as evidence of facts or events

report (*n*)   an account or announcement that is prepared, presented, or delivered, usually in formal or organized form

research and development (*n*)   study and investigation of new products and processes

resignation (*n*)   the act of giving up a position or office; a written statement declaring one's intention to resign

résumé (*n*)   a summary of one's educational background and employment record submitted with a job application

retail department (*n*)   a department which is in charge of selling goods in small quantities to the consumer (the department in charge of selling goods in large quantities is the *wholesale department*)

retire (*v*)   to withdraw from business, public life, or active service

retirement (*n*)   the act or state of being retired

salary (*n*)   a fixed amount of money for work that is done, paid on a regular basis

sales department (*n*)   division of a company in charge of selling

sales manager (*n*)   person in charge of selling and sales policies

salespeople (*n*)   people hired to sell merchandise in a store or in a designated territory

sales personnel (*n*)   salespeople and other staff working in a sales department

sales report (*n*)   an account or statement describing a company's sales for a given period of time

sales representative (*n*)   a salesperson

saturation campaign (*n*)   a very intense advertising campaign

secretary (*n*)   a person employed to handle correspondence, keep files, and do clerical work in an office or for an individual; (also *administrative assistant*)

semiskilled labor (*n*)   work which does not require much specialized ability or training

senior executive (*n*)   an executive who is highest in rank

shareholder (*n*)   an owner of a share or shares of a company's stock; a stockholder

shipment (*n*)   the act of sending goods by any means of transportation

shipping department (*n*)   a division in a company in charge of the shipment or receipt of goods

shop (*n*)   plant or small factory

shop steward (*n*)   a union member chosen by fellow workers to represent them in their dealings with the management

shop supervisor (*n*)   person in charge of a shop

skilled craftsman (*n*)   a trained worker; an artisan

staff (*n*)   personnel of a business or organization

statement (*n*)   a report of a commercial or financial account showing an amount due, a bill; a monthly report sent to a debtor or bank depositor

statistics (*n*)   a collection of numerical data

steward (*n*)   see *shop steward*

stockroom (*n*)   a room in which goods or materials are stored

strategy (*n*)   a planned technique for obtaining a result (e.g., sales strategy)

strike (*n*)   a cessation of work by employees to obtain certain demands from the employer, such as higher pay or improved conditions

study (*n*)   a report prepared after researching a particular subject

supervisor (*n*)   a person who supervises or directs and inspects the performance of workers or work

supply room (*n*)   a stockroom usually for materials used in an office

survey (*n*)   a detailed inspection or investigation

tailor-made (*adj*)   made according to specific needs or preferences; made to order

tax deductible (*adj*)   exempt from inclusion in one's taxable income

tax investment credit (*n*)   an amount legally deductible from a person's or a company's taxable income to encourage investment

team (*n*)   a group of people working together for a similar cause

terms (*n*)   conditions

territory (*n*)   the area for which a person is responsible as representative or agent

trade (*n*)   an occupation, especially one requiring skilled labor; commerce

trade fair (*n*)   a fair organized to promote the sale of goods or products (see *fair*)

trade journal (*n*)   a magazine published regularly by a particular business or industry to give pertinent news and developments

Trade Mission (*n*)   a government agency set up in a foreign country to promote commerce with that country

trade union (*n*)   an association of workers in the same trade organized to improve working conditions; a labor union

transit (*n*)   the conveyance of persons or goods from one point to another

union (*n*)   a labor union; an alliance for mutual interest or benefit

vacancy (*n*)   an opening for employment

warehouse (*n*)   a storehouse for goods or merchandise

white-collar (*adj*)   of or pertaining to workers whose work usually does not involve manual labor and who are expected to dress with some degree of formality

work experience (*n*)   a person's experience in a particular field or job